A Superior High Priest

A Concise Commentary on the Epistle to the Hebrews

By

L. S. Watkins

Disclaimer

The author of this work has quoted the writers of many articles and books. This does not mean that the author endorses or recommends the works of others. If the author quotes someone, it does not mean that he agrees with all the author's tenets, statements, concepts, or words, whether in the work quoted or any other work of the author. There has been no attempt to alter the meaning of the quotes; and therefore, some of the quotes are long to give the entire sense of the passage.

REL067030: Religion: Christian Theology - Apologetics

ISBN 979-8-9890422-8-9

Published 12/09/23

All Scripture quotes are from the King James Bible except those verses compared and then the source is identified.

Address All Inquiries To:
THE OLD PATHS PUBLICATIONS, INC.
142 Gold Flume Way
Cleveland, Georgia, U.S.A.

Web: www.theoldpathspublications.com
E-mail: TOP@theoldpathspublications.com

1.0

DEDICATION

To my beautiful wife and children, my first pastor and spiritual father, Dr. Allen Jones, and to all who show up to hear my ramblings week after week.

ACKNOWLEDGMENTS:

The author wishes to thank God for His innumerable blessings and for revealing any Scriptural truth that can be found within these pages. Thanks go to the author's wife, Jessie, for sparing time and offering much support, encouragement, and valuable criticism (Pro. 31:10). Thanks also to Pastor William Burrows for many things, but especially the support and suggestion of Dr. Jones for the Foreword. Dr. Jones is to be thanked for having written such a complimentary Foreword despite his intense schedule. Thanks to Pastor Stephen Chronister for all the time on the phone and for making this author find the answers instead of handing them out. Thank you to Eunice Brown for her excellent and tireless work on the project. Thanks to all those who encouraged the writing of this monograph, including, but not limited to, Claudia Watkins (Mom) and Jeremy Stevens. Finally, thank you to Dr. H.D. Williams and his wife for all the hard work and long hours and for following the Lord in founding and operating T.O.P., and to Dr. Steve Combs for sending me in their direction.

FOREWORD

Brother Lucas S. Watkins has certainly done a spectacular job in his <u>A Superior High Priest</u>. In the opening portion of his work, he stated his purpose to disclose Christ as better or Christ as superior. This purpose is adhered to throughout the book as he not only writes of Christ's finished work excelling the transactions of the Mosaic Law, but the "finished" meaning exactly that. The Law, no matter how strictly it was carried out, could never reach the plateau of acceptance with God for salvation as the author proves over and over with scriptural evidence. When Christ said, *"It is finished"* (Jn. 19:30), this is precisely what took place. All the Law could do was keep those under it reminded of their sins as they were to continue coming with the sacrifices demanded. The author does well in pointing this out in contrast to Christ's entering *"...once in the holy place..."* (Heb. 9:12), never to be repeated. He also shows how Christ *"...after he had offered one sacrifice for sins forever, sat down..."* Heb. 10:12), something the priest of the Old Testament was never privileged to do because his work was never completed.

Many other contrasts the author makes to reveal the superiority of Christ. These consist of Christ's words, His way, His worth and much more. He reveals Christ to be the example believers should follow in taking up their cross daily and following Him. The author portrays Christ's prayer life and His yielding to God's will; that even though as man He had a will and that man's will must yield to God's.

His emphasis on the blood is very important. He shows the fallacy of discounting the value of Christ's blood and embracing His death over it. To the Israelites in Egypt, God did not give the message, "When I see the slain carcasses of the animals, I will pass over you, but *"...when I see the blood, I will pass over you..."* (Ex. 12:13). The word "blood" is found more times in Hebrews than any other book in the New Testament.

The author is to be commended for his grasp on the purpose for the letter to the Hebrews. Dr. Carpenter, my most revered professor, said one day in Bible class, "Paul wrote to the Hebrews to tell them to stop being Hebrews." My study of Hebrews convinced me, the key thought is *"Let us go on to perfection..."* (Heb. 6:1). Brother Watkins even though he pursues his quest of the Superior Christ, never veers from the need for maturity of the Hebrew believers. This undoubtedly is, if not the major problem in our churches, one that is very high on the list. The work of the Superior Christ has made available to the believer all that is necessary for his maturity.

Brother Watkins resolutely refutes false concepts and addresses misunderstandings of biblical truths in the kindest manner while never approaching either apart from scriptural support or scholarly input as his bibliography reveals. Having been in the ministry for fifty plus years, easily comprehended is the manner of his time in the study and time spent in prayer. Be sure and read his Excurses 1 and 2. They seal much of the truths found in this work.

Brother Watkins is my junior in ministry, age, and experience in excess of forty years; however, I am reminded of a comment given by Dr. Grant Carter in one of our Bible classes at the International Baptist Bible Institute, "Truth is truth, no matter who says it or where it is found." There is quite a difference in truth from the Bible and a Bible truth. Truth from the Bible can and is given many times out of context. A Bible truth is keeping that truth in context, or in other words, "rightly divided" in what the Scripture teaches elsewhere on the subject.

There are more than forty works on the book of Hebrews in my library, counting the single volumes, plus commentaries. This work by Lucas Watkins is valued among the best of them.

James Jones, Jr.
Harriman, Tennessee
12/09/23

TABLE OF CONTENTS

INTRODUCTION

"If you do not attempt to imitate Paul in anything else as to preaching, be sure to follow his example in this-that you try to adapt every sermon to that time, that place, that people;..."[1]

The book of Hebrews has been described as "the document of faith,"[2] by G. Campbell Morgan, and "the sweet harmony of both Testaments,"[3] by John Flavel, and is said to "set forth the finality of Christ's salvation. . .,"[4] by Dr. Merrill Unger. Albert Barnes called it "the most important part of the New Testament."[5] According to William Barclay, "there is no book in the New Testament which is more worth the effort to understand."[6]

It is also one of the most disputed. Because they are not mentioned directly in the book itself, some items in dispute have been and are:

(1) authorship,
(2) time of writing,
(3) place of writing,

---

[1] Broadus, John A. *The History of Preaching* (A.C. Armstrong & Son, 1889), p. 41.

[2] Morgan, G. Campbell *The Triumph of Faith* (Revell, 1944), p. 15.

[3] Flavel, John, *The Fountain of Life* (American Tract Society), p. 11.

[4] Unger, Merrill F., *Unger's Bible Handbook* (Moody Press, 1966), p. 747.

[5] Barnes, Albert, *Notes on the New Testament-Hebrews* (Baker Book House, Grand Rapids, 1951), 3.

[6] Barclay, William, *The Letter to the Hebrews* (The Westminster Press, Philadelphia, 1957), ix of the foreword.

(4) to whom it was written specifically,
(5) the original language in which it was written,
(6) its purpose, and
(7) its canonicity, i.e., does it belong in Scripture?

We will briefly look at some evidence for the more important questions: Authorship, time of writing, and purpose, and will take it for granted that it belongs in the canon of Scripture.

Authorship

The authorship of the book of Hebrews has been in dispute since the earliest times. Those who would know (the 1st c. Jews to whom it was written) remain tight-lipped…

Some guesses as to authorship are: the disciple Luke, the apostle Paul, not Paul (Jerome, Augustine, Calvin), Apollos (Luther), Barnabas (Tertullian), Priscilla and/or Aquila (Harnack), Peter, Clement of Rome, etc. Any candidate for the author (as he shall be called throughout this book, except in some quotations) must meet these requirements:

(1) Was a male.[7]
(2) Was highly educated in Jewish religion, scripture (O.T.), and history. One might say a 'Hebrew of Hebrews.'
(3) Was Jewish himself (1:2).
(4) Had an immense burden for his Jewish brethren.

---

[7] Fruchtenbaum, Arnold G., *Ariel's Bible Commentary-The Messianic Jewish Epistles* (Ariel Ministries, 2005), p. 165.

(5) Was a companion of Timothy (13:23).

(6) Was alive while the Temple still functioned (10:11), so between Christ's ascension and the Temple's destruction in A.D. 70.[8]

(7) Suffered imprisonment for his Christian witness (10:34).

(8) Some fair and early extra-Biblical support regarding authorship. The testimony from the earliest Greek 'fathers' should carry more weight than the Alexandrian or Latin ones. Sir Robert Anderson writes:

> "Due weight has never been given to this fact in estimating the value of the general testimony of the Greek Fathers that the writer was the Apostle Paul. To attribute equal value to the statements of certain Latin Fathers of a later date betrays ignorance of the science of evidence."[9]

He also points out that there exists a certain hermeneutical(interpretational) bias that caused many Roman Catholic 'fathers' to cast doubt on the authenticity of the book of Hebrews.[10] This bias is still held today by the leadership of the Roman Catholic Church as well as many 'Protestant' churches and its most popular iteration is found in the 'Replacement theology' of many Reformed churches. This will be examined in some detail, but

---

[8] Wuest, Kenneth S., *Hebrews in the Greek New Testament* (Wm. B. Eerdmans Publishing Company, 1947), p. 14.

[9] Anderson, Sir Robert, *Types In Hebrews* (Kregel Publications, Grand Rapids, 1978), p. 11.

[10] Ibid, pp. 2-3.

for now, understand that the men who hold this view believe that the 'Church' has replaced Israel in God's program of events, and that God has forsaken Israel. Why then would the Holy Spirit inspire an entire book to Hebrews that says anything but "God has forsaken you, sorry about your luck!"?

(9) It would also be really helpful if there was some hint somewhere in the Bible itself that a writing full of wisdom had been sent to Jewish Christians, especially if it were to name the author of such a work by name (See 2 Peter 3:15)!

By now it should be clear that Paul the apostle is the clear favorite. So, does Paul himself give us any clue? Paul said that his 'epistles' had a special mark, a token:

> *"The salutation of Paul with mine own hand, which is the token in every epistle: so I write. The grace of our Lord Jesus Christ be with you all. Amen."*
> II Thessalonians 3:17-18

Paul says here that his letters bear a mark or 'token' as evidence of his authorship.

Because we are used to the western style of correspondence, our 'salutation' occurs at the very beginning of our letters. Modern writers see that Paul does not identify himself at the beginning of Hebrews and say "Aha!" but it should be noticed that Paul's letters always *end* with salutations (Romans 16, 1 Corinthians 16, etc., etc.).

Without exception, some form of "grace be with you." occurs at the end of every Pauline epistle, and at the end of Hebrews.

Consider also the heart-wrenching burden Paul had for his brethren, the Jews. In Romans 9:33 we read:

"For I could wish that myself were accursed from Christ for my brethren, my kinsmen according to the flesh:"

He also ends up ignoring the Holy Spirit's warning against going to Jerusalem in Acts 19-21, his burden being so heavy.

Some have objected to Paul's authorship of Hebrews on the basis of style. A careful reading of Acts, however, will show that Paul tailored his oratorical style based on his audience.

These speeches in Acts sound much like Hebrews because Paul is addressing Hebrews.

"For if the word spoken by angels was stedfast, and every transgression and disobedience received a just recompence of reward;" 2:2

"Men and brethren, children of the stock of Abraham, and whosoever among you feareth God, to you is the word of this salvation sent."

"God hath fulfilled the same unto us their children, in that he hath raised up Jesus again; as it is also written in the second

psalm, Thou art my Son, this day have I begotten thee." Acts 13:26,33.

Many believe the thirteenth chapter could have been written by Paul, even if the rest wasn't.[11] Some have suggested that he wrote the first twelve chapters early on, and the thirteenth later. This argument is based, not only on style, but a certain private interpretation they hold which will be addressed later (See Excursus 1).

If Paul did indeed write the book of Hebrews, why would he not identify himself right out of the gate like he did in the Pauline epistles? Here are some possibilities:

(1) This book is not a letter like the other epistles, but a theological treatise.
(2) The treatise had to be carried into dangerous territory, as Paul's preaching had caused civil unrest in the empire, and tensions between Rome and both the Jews and Christians were reaching a crescendo. A message bearing his name might have been confiscated or might even put the carrier at great peril.
(3) The letter and carrier would have faced danger from the non-believing Jews as well, who still taught Christ to be a heretic.[12]
(4) He may not have carried the same clout with Jews as he did elsewhere as he was the

---

[11] Ruckman, Peter S., *The Book of Hebrews* (self-published, 1986), preface, xvii.
[12] Gaebelein, A.C., *The Annotated Bible: Phil-Hebrews* (Our Hope, 1917), p. 229.

'Apostle to the Gentiles' (Romans 11:13). His name may have been an immediate turn-off.
(5) Perhaps Paul wanted rather to emphasize the One Whose name *does* appear at the beginning: God (1:1).

All this being said, complete certainty cannot be maintained. Both Barnabas and Apollos also meet many of the criteria mentioned above (Jewish, mighty in Scripture, etc.). The most conservative commentators tend toward Paul, while the more liberal seem completely averse. One thing is absolutely certain: the Holy Spirit is truly the Author, and the human author was the instrument.

II Timothy 3:16:

"All scripture is given by inspiration of God..."

Setting

Because the addressees are not named anywhere in the body of this book, there is a question as to whom exactly it is written. It is, however, undeniably clear that it is written to Jewish people, and its writing precedes the siege of Jerusalem, and the destruction of the Temple in A.D. 70. This information is critical to understanding some of the more controversial passages found therein. Some have said that the phrase in Chapter 13 *"They of Italy salute you"* means the Jews in Rome were meant.[13] Some good

---

[13] Exell, Rev. Joseph S., *The Biblical Expositor-Hebrews Vol. 1* (James Nisbet & Co., London), Intro., ix-x.

points are made in this respect. Paul writing from Rome also makes a lot of sense.

Theme

Knowing the theme of the book of the Bible you are reading is always helpful. It keeps you in mind of what the author's point in writing is. In the case of Hebrews, it is more important than any other book we can think of. This writer was listening to another pastor's preparatory remarks as he was introducing an expository series on this book, and he gave the theme as "Warnings Against Apostacy in Trying Times." While there are dire warnings in the book for the 1st century Jewish Christians, and their situation parallels what it looks like Christians may be experiencing in the near future, making the warnings the theme puts the focus somewhere other than where it ought to be. Besides that, the warnings have no strength if they are not tied together by the theme! The series ended up being a diatribe about Lordship Salvation.

There is one theme that each of the books of the Bible points to, however indirectly. Paul's epistles all relate to Christian living, but the Christian life cannot be lived outside of Christ. "What about the historical books of the Old Testament?" you say. Whether you recognize it or not, EVERY book is about Christ. The historical books are about the history of redemption, and therefore have their central theme as Christ. If you want some authority on the issue, take a spin on this:

Jesus said in John 5:39:

"Search the scriptures; for in them ye think ye have eternal life: and they are they which testify of me."

Jesus says the Scriptures testify of Him. In the preface to the King James Bible, there is a section in the prefatory material that tells about the canonization process. This is the process by which it was determined which books should be included in the Bible. This writer is very thankful that the final verdict was never up to single men, councils, or even scholars, because the book of Hebrews rarely made this list. Men as imminent as Luther didn't think it belonged. Yet it speaks of Christ in a way no other book can come close to. It is the strongest link between the anticipatory nature of the religion of the Jewish people, and the satisfaction of Christ's fulfilling work.

The proper theme, therefore, is "Christ is better," or "Christ is Superior." This theme is not only repeated throughout the book but is the answer to the warnings found in it. The author tells his audience to be strong and not go back to Judaism. Why? Because Christ is Superior. The old religion was God-ordained and served its purpose but does no longer. Why? Because Christ is Superior. In the old religion, God's people could never enter His presence. They couldn't go into the Most Holy Place. Only the priest could, and that once a year. But now, in Christ, the believer has access to the very presence of God, any time he or she needs. Why? Because Christ is Superior. No person or church should be able to persuade the Christian into any kind of works-based system of religion. Outward religion is obsolete. Why? Because Christ is Superior!

Keeping Christ as the theme will keep the guardrails up regarding interpretation. It will also guard against apostasy. If Christ is the theme, you won't force the Bible into extreme versions of Dispensationalism. If Christ is the theme, then the passages that appear to let on that salvation can be lost will be understood. If Christ's salvation can be lost, how is Christ Superior? We refer again to II Peter 3:15-16.

> *"And account that the longsuffering of our Lord is salvation; even as our beloved brother Paul also according to the wisdom given unto him hath written unto you; As also in all his epistles, speaking in them of these things; in which are some things hard to be understood, which they that are unlearned and unstable wrest, as they do also the other scriptures, unto their own destruction."*

We assure you, this book, along with Matthew, Acts, and James are the most wrested down to this modern day. In this book, we will put 'Wresting' in contrast to 'Resting,' which is one of the subthemes of the book of Hebrews.

One final word about the theme. The theme is sister to the setting. Hebrews is very confusing to many because

(1) they don't know that it is written to people who are facing possible judgment,

(2) and who would immediately understand the Old Testament references and allusions, and

(3) whose conversion was fundamentally different from most others. They didn't come to Christ from the darkness of paganism. They weren't irreligious. They had the right religion until one day they didn't. New Light was shed that added a piece that had been missing for 1,900 years. And not just 'a' piece. *The* Missing Piece (or 'Peace'). This makes a difference for interpreting this wonderful book.

Scope

There is a third key to bringing this book into the light of understanding. Unfortunately for us, this key is another confusing book. We don't often agree with Augustine (of Hippo), but on this point, we believe him to be right. The key to Hebrews is Leviticus. The key to Leviticus is…Hebrews! We will go to significant lengths to show how the priestly themes found in this third sister will open up the Scripture to us. For the 1st century Jew, the book is an admonishment to go from the shadow to the substance, the good things of Judaism to the better things of Christ, from the earthly Temple to the Heavenly sanctuary, from the conditional promises of the Old Covenant to the unconditional promises of the New, and from the incompleteness of the old dispensation to the completeness of the new.[14]

---

[14] Taken primarily from Ironside, Harry A., *Hebrews and Titus* (Loizeaux Bros., 1932), pp. 14-15.

Application

There is some truth to the idea that reading Hebrews is like reading someone else's mail. The original readers would have been a bit different from us and would have been facing special circumstances. There is also a special place for Hebrews as we believe it will be the second witness to the preaching of the tribulation period and will be the most natural guide for the Jewish people of that great day. Remember, they won't have years to study the entire New Testament, and the warnings will nearly perfectly parallel what they will face. We do not believe, however, that the teachings in this book cannot be applied to Christians today. We do not believe it teaches another way of salvation. As we progress, we will keep in mind the theme and keys and see that this book teaches Christ and Christ alone for salvation. Eternal security is in every chapter, if not every paragraph, of the book to the Hebrews.

HEBREWS CHAPTER 1

". . .pure gold is not recognized by itself; but when we test it along with baser ore, we perceive which is the better." -Artabanus[15]

> *"God, who at sundry times and in divers manners spake in time past unto the fathers by the prophets, Hath in these last days spoken unto us by his Son,"*
> Hebrews 1:1,2a

Instead of introducing himself, the author of this book places the emphasis where it ought to be- on God. In fact, "...Few NT books speak of God so often."[16] Several of the commentators reviewed gave the Greek word order, which this writer found completely unhelpful. Far more helpful are the many comparisons that are drawn between this prologue and the others found in scripture. The first occurs at the very beginning:

> *"In the beginning God created the heaven and the earth."* Genesis 1:1

The next opens the book of John:

> *"In the beginning was the Word, and the Word was with God, and the Word was God. The same was in the beginning with God. All things were made by him; and without him was not any thing made that was*

---

[15] Rawlinson, George, trans. *The History of Herodotus* (Taylor Publishing Company, 1956), p. 359.

[16] Morris, Leon, *Hebrews-Revelation*, vol. 12 of *The Expositor's Bible Commentary*, p. 12.

made. In him was life; and the life was the light of men. And the light shineth in darkness; and the darkness comprehended it not." John 1:1-5

Genesis 1:1 is the beginning of the work of God in Creation. John 1:1-5 is the beginning of work of Christ in Creation *and* revelation. Hebrews 1:1-2 is the history of the work of God in Creation, revelation, and finally redemption.

The purpose of this introduction makes perfect sense when the intended audience and the theme are kept in mind. The writer wishes to reinforce the tie between 'the God' (their well-known Jehovah) and the late revelation of Christ. Christ IS that God! This would be a natural first step in the process of admonishing anxious people who are facing persecution and reminding them of the surety of this relationship when the persecutors are jailing and even killing them for this belief.

The purpose of the written Word, the Bible is the to reveal what God wants man to know. Chafer said,

> "Like a telescope, the Bible reaches beyond the stars and penetrates the heights of heaven and the depths of hell. Like a microscope, it discovers the minutest details of God's plan and purpose as well as the hidden secrets of the human heart. Like a stereoscope, it has the capacity to place things in their right relation the one to the other, manifesting the true perspective of the divine intent in the universe. So far as human

knowledge goes, the Bible deals as freely with the things unknown as it does with the known. It speaks with the utmost freedom and assurance of things altogether outside the range of human life and experience-of things eternal as well as of time. There is a border beyond which the human mind, basing its conclusions on experience, cannot go; yet the human authors of the Bible did not hesitate when they reached that boundary, but moved majestically on into unknown realms with intrepidity. By what other means than through the Bible may one gaze into eternity, either backward or forward? Yet the theory that the Bible does not originate in God alone, imposes the necessity of believing that restricted and temporal creatures of the Earth have themselves arisen to the sublime conceptions of eternity and of heaven as well as to the eternal Being of God, and are able to sit in judgment over the eternal destiny of all things. Man could not write such a Book if he would."[17]

The main thrust of the written revelation is the story of God's redemptive work through Christ. This story is played out in stages. This makes the revelation progressive.

Hebrews 1:1 states very clearly that God's revelation to mankind has come in various forms,

---

[17] Chafer, Lewis Sperry, *Systematic Theology,* (Dallas Theological Seminary, 1947), Vol. I, p. 27.

and not all at the same time. This is a critical interpretational maxim that is commonly called 'progressive revelation,' or, "the recognition that God's message to man was not given in one single act but was unfolded in a long series of successive acts..."[18]

Charles Hodge said,

"The progressive character of divine revelation is recognized in relation to all the great doctrines of the Bible... What at first is only obscurely intimated is gradually unfolded in subsequent parts of the sacred volume, until the truth is revealed in its fulness."[19]

And Thomas Constable:

"His means included types, symbols, commandments, precepts, warnings, exhortations, visions, dreams, signs, parables, events, and face-to-face visitations."[20]

For some examples:

Adam and Eve

Federal headship demonstrated (Eve sinned, but it was Adam's responsibility, and

---

[18] Ryrie, Charles C., *Dispensationalism Today* (Moody Press, 1965), p. 33.

[19] Hodge, Charles, *Systematic Theology,* Vol. 1 (Hendrickson Publishers, 2020), p. 446.

[20] Constable, Thomas, *Notes on Hebrews,* 2023 Kindle Edition. pp. 17-18.

Adam's sin was the one that affected successive generations).

Blood/death required, covering of shame required, works not accepted (the fig-leaf coverings weren't sufficient).

Cain and Abel

Atonement, blood required.

Enoch

God coming to Earth in judgment. (Second Advent). Jude 14,15.

Abraham

Introduction of and plan for God's chosen people, righteousness credited by faith (Genesis 12, Genesis 15:6).

Moses

God's name, YHVH (Jehovah). Exodus 6:3 Passover, etc. Law Exodus 20. Pictures of Christ in Leviticus through sacrifices, priesthood, ark of the testimony, etc.

Although this specific text (Hebrews 1:1) is speaking specifically about the messages from God through the prophets, the concept is there. God had spoken to men with words, now He will speak through the Word that became flesh (John 1:1-5 above).

And so on until the final revelation came. *"Hath in these last days spoken unto us by his Son,"* (verse 2 of the text).

There was the testimony of the words of God, followed by the Word that was God, followed by the Word of God.

"But when that which is perfect is come, then that which is in part shall be done away." I Corinthians 13:10

"We have also a more sure word of prophecy; whereunto ye do well that ye take heed, as unto a light that shineth in a dark place, until the day dawn, and the day star arise in your hearts:" II Peter 1:19

The permanency of revelation:

"The secret things belong unto the LORD our God: but those things which are revealed belong unto us and to our children for ever, that we may do all the words of this law." Deuteronomy 29:29

Everything that God is going to reveal about the redemptive story has been revealed in the Person of Christ. Everything is fulfilled.

This is the final major piece: Once something has been revealed, it can't be unrevealed. Once God has given man a revelation concerning Himself, it stays in place forever. The cat never goes back into the bag. This will also be critical to the interpretation of this book.

So, to review:

(1) Progressive revelation means God releases His revelations at different times throughout history.

(2) Progressive revelation may modify the CONTENT of the Gospel, never its object.

(3) Once something is revealed, it can never be unrevealed.

Some final notes on progressive revelation:

(1) Covenants always reveal something about God, but revelation obviously does not always come in the form of a covenant. Covenants often relate to one man, or one group and are always limited to God's elect (people He chose for a redemptive purpose, not to be saved individually), not all of mankind (men are offered the New Covenant of the Church, but none are included until they agree to the requirements, and the covenant kicks in-a time still future). The attempt to make everything God does a covenant is a hallmark of Covenant Theology.

(2) Dispensations are sometimes based on progressive revelation, but the revelations do not always start a new dispensation.

Progressive revelation is sometimes related to soteriology (salvation), but it is critical to know that the means of escaping condemnation is always grace through faith. Progressive revelation may change the content of the Gospel message (you didn't have to believe in the resurrection of Christ before He was resurrected), but the object in which you place that faith (God) remains the same.

"Hath in these last days"

Because of the Greek root word of 'last' (ἐσχατος, or eschatos), there is some controversy about which time period is specified here, but if you take the English expression 'last days' everywhere it occurs in the Bible, it becomes clear that the 'last days' began with Christ's ministry and will end with the conclusion of the Millennial reign.

"And Jacob called unto his sons, and said, Gather yourselves together, that I may tell you that which shall befall you in the last days." Genesis 49:1

"And it shall come to pass in the last days, that the mountain of the LORD'S house shall be established in the top of the mountains, and shall be exalted above the hills; and all nations shall flow unto it." Isaiah 2:2

"But in the last days it shall come to pass, that the mountain of the house of the LORD shall be established in the top of the mountains, and it shall be exalted above the hills; and people shall flow unto it." Micah 4:1

"And it shall come to pass in the last days, saith God, I will pour out of my Spirit upon all flesh: and your sons and your daughters shall prophesy, and your young

men shall see visions, and your old men shall dream dreams:" Acts 2:17

"This know also, that in the last days perilous times shall come."
II Timothy 2:1

"Your gold and silver is cankered; and the rust of them shall be a witness against you, and shall eat your flesh as it were fire. Ye have heaped treasure together for the last days." James 5:3

"Knowing this first, that there shall come in the last days scoffers, walking after their own lusts," II Peter 3:3

And, just for effect,

"And this is the will of him that sent me, that every one which seeth the Son, and believeth on him, may have everlasting life: and I will raise him up at the last day." John 6:40

This is the final resurrection. Also, for those who think that three thousand (two thousand since Christ, plus the Millennium) years' worth of days (just over a million) is too many last days,

"But, beloved, be not ignorant of this one thing, that one day is with the Lord as a thousand years, and a thousand years as one day." II Peter 3:8

The 'last days' are only three days in God's calendar.

> *"...his Son, whom he hath appointed
> heir of all things,"* v. 2b

The part of the Bible we refer to as the New Testament is a record of the speaking God did by His Son, the Lord Jesus Christ, and the church He founded, including the rules of its practice and its future. The idea that the author puts forth of Christ being God's mouthpiece (or better, God's mouth) is a claim Christ Himself made while bodily present on Earth.

> *"No man hath seen God at any time;
> the only begotten Son, which is in the bosom
> of the Father, he hath declared him."* John 1:18

If you count *'his Son'* from verse 1, there are seven references to Christ as the Son in Hebrews, and this small section lists seven aspects of His unique greatness.[21] It is then followed by seven Old Testament quotations that prove His superiority over angels. More may be said of the nature of Christ's Sonship when it is further discussed later in the book of Hebrews, but it should be enough for now to say that the Divine plan of the Godhead prior to the Creation was that this second Member of the Triunity should assume a Son-to-Father relationship for the purposes of eternal redemption. Eminent theologians of various stripes revel in a pair of sister doctrines known as the 'eternal generation of the Son' and 'eternal subordination.' In this writer's opinion, the former can be excused on the basis of intellectual

---

[21] Constable, *Hebrews*, pp. 19-20.

pragmatism (an incomplete understanding of God's timelessness-a trait every human shares), however the second is rank Arian heresy, though they will deny it.

The text says God appointed Christ as heir of all things. Here is a short list of some things Christ stands to inherit.

(1) The kingdoms of the world-Revelation 11:15, I Corinthians 15:25, Psalm 110:1
(2) The kingdom of heaven- Matthew 6:13
(3) The saints- John 6:37,
(4) The fruit the saints produce-Matthew 21, Mark 12, Luke 20, Ephesians 1:8
(5) Everything we inherit, as we are joint-heirs-Romans 8:17
(6) The entire cosmos (visible and invisible) as He died to redeem everything God created that sin ruined- our text.

It will be seen in chapter 2 of this book that Christ won a right to His inheritance *by obedience*. He was God's Son, sinless, the God-man, but these only qualified Him for service. It is on the basis of His service that He inherits. He earned it. No cross, no inheritance. There are things we stand to inherit based on His work, but there are rewards that can be gained or lost dependent on our service (I Corinthians 3:15, James 1:12, Revelation 2:10 and 3:11).

Revelation 11:15 above describes the point in time when Christ will be given the kingdoms of the world to reign over in fulfillment of the Davidic Covenant, foretold in Genesis 49:10, and put into words (promised) in II Samuel 7:8-16. This period lasts 1000 years which is why it is called the Millennial Reign of Christ. God will keep His promise!

"by whom also he made the worlds;" v. 2c

This statement simply means that Christ was the direct agent of Creation. God, in the Person of Christ created the world. The underlying word "αἰὼν" or "aion" is where we get our word eon, or an epoch of time. This causes confusion for those who aren't content with the perfect Word we have in our hands. The 'worlds' are everything and everyone in space *and* time.[22] Think about 2 Peter 3:8, where he says, *'the world that then was.'* This is the world before the Flood. Europe was the 'Old World', America the 'New.' The world refers to people in general, lost people, the world system, domains, planets, etc. This writer can't think of a better way to say in one word, "God's creation" than "worlds."

We refer once again to one of our cross references, the prologue to the book of John:

> *"All things were made by him (the Word, Jesus Christ); and without him was not any thing made that was made."* John 1:3

Many commentators could be cited to support the idea that the 'him' of this verse is indeed Jesus Christ, but our favorite is by Adam Clarke:

---

[22] Wuest, (quoting Alford), *Hebrews*, p. 36.

"…Christ and the Father are One. To say that Christ made all things by a delegated power from God is absurd; because the thing is impossible…this is…a work that can only be done by omnipotence. Now, God cannot delegate his omnipotence to another…for it is impossible that there should be two omnipotent beings." (Italics removed)[23]

Jesus Christ, as God, created everything. That means before anything else existed, there was God, and He was Christ. You don't have to believe it, but the Bible does say it.[24] It's also the only Biblically logical conclusion as well, as seen in this quote:

"Either *creatio ex nihilo* (creation from nothing) is true, or God did not create everything…if matter is eternal and God could not create without it, this would be a limit on God's power…Therefore we can assert: 'Either *creatio ex nihilo* is true, or God is not all-powerful…God's being all-powerful strongly suggests creation out of nothing.'"[25]

Copan and Craig also say:

---

[23] Clarke, Adam, *Clarke's Commentary Vol V.* (Abingdon), p. 512.

[24] This is not an affirmation of 'Oneness doctrine,' but a declaration of Christ's deity. Christ is a Person of the Trinity.

[25] Copan, Paul and Craig, *Creation Out of Nothing* (Baker Academic, 2004), p. 91.

> "If matter were uncreated, then it would from the very first be of a rank equal to God and would deserve the same veneration."[26]

Saying Christ is 'before all things' places Him before and above Creation, and separate from it, for before the Creation, only God exists. Also, if Christ is Creator, He cannot be created as the Jehovah's Witness would claim.

This phrase at the end of verse 2 is tied to another in verse 3, so if you'll allow it, we wish to move forward out of order for a moment:

"and upholding all things by the word of his power," v. 3b

An apt cross reference to this verse is Colossians 1:16 and 17:

> "For by him were all things created, that are in heaven, and that are in earth, visible and invisible, whether they be thrones, or dominions, or principalities, or powers: all things were created by him, and for him: And he is before all things, and by him all things consist."

These are two separate ideas. Not only did Christ create all worlds, but He upholds them by the word of His power. His word also determines the program of the ages, commonly called 'dispensations.' This puts to rest the maxim of the Deist which says that (their) God created the universe, wound it up like a clock, then stepped

---

26 Copan and Craig, *Creation*, p. 15.

away and is now watching it unwind. He is actively involved in every atom of His creation at every moment of time. This should bring the Christian great peace. Here's some food for thought:

Our known universe has been calculated to contain a hundred million trillion trillion trillion trillion trillion trillion elementary particles (10^{80}).[27] As an act of creation, this statistic, if accurate, is truly impressive, and displays how far beyond us Christ's omnipotence is.

What is being addressed here is creation *and* conservation. Christ not only originated the entire universe, but continues, every moment, to hold every elementary particle of it in His power. According to Norman Geisler, He "not only controls what comes to exist or continues to exist, but He directs the very course of things that do exist."[28] This displays His omnipotence *and* His omniscience simultaneously, for how can He hold every atom together if He doesn't know where each one is?

To Christ Jesus belongs all glory, power, honor, and praise!

> *"Who being the brightness of his glory, and the express image of his person, and upholding all things by the word of his power,"* v. 3a-b

---

[27] Swenson, Richard A., *More Than Meets the Eye* (NavPress, 2000), p. 142.

[28] Geisler, Norman, "God Knows All" in *Predestination & Free Will,* ed. David and Randall Basinger (InterVarsity Press, 1986), p. 64.

'The brightness of his glory' means that God's glory appeared on Earth in the form of Christ; not reflecting the brightness, not *in* the brightness. THE brightness. 'The express image of His person' means that Christ, in His divine nature, manifested Himself in human form, and it made a physical copy that was human. He is not said to be made *in* the image of God, like Adam in Genesis 1:27, but that He *is* the image of God. So, we have God's glory, veiled in human flesh, though a glimpse of that glory shone through at the mount of transfiguration.

> *"Jesus saith unto him, Have I been so long time with you, and yet hast thou not known me, Philip? he that hath seen me hath seen the Father; and how sayest thou then, Shew us the Father?"* John 14:9

> *"when he had by himself purged our sins, sat down on the right hand of the Majesty on high;"* v. 3c

A crucial, yet oft overlooked phrase is *'by himself.'* In the book of John, chapters 7, 8, and 13, Jesus tells His disciples that He is going away, and they would seek Him and not find Him. Then He tells them that where He is going, they cannot go. Jesus Christ was the <u>only One</u> Who could go to the cross and accomplish what He did. He was the only sinless One. He was the only God-man. Only He was qualified. Similarly, the Old Testament priests could not be just anyone. They had to qualify genetically, physically, and by sanctification. This makes both the office of the priests and the office of Christ, our Priest unique. Only Christ could purge our sins. Only Christ could satisfy the Father. Only Christ could place His blood on the heavenly mercy seat. Like Christ, the high priest went into the most holy place *by himself*.

The last phrase *"and sat down at the right hand of the Majesty on high;"* speaks of the fact that when Jesus arose and ascended to the Father, His redemptive work was finished. There was nothing left to do. He accomplished salvation BY HIMSELF. There is no need for another sacrifice or priest. There is no more sacrificing Christ at every Mass.

The right hand is the place reserved for Christ, and He sits there until the Millennium begins. At that time, He will sit on the throne of David in Jerusalem.

> *"The LORD said unto my Lord, Sit thou at my right hand, until I make thine enemies thy footstool."* Psalm 110:1

> *"Hereafter shall the Son of man sit on the right hand of the power of God."* Luke 22:69

> *"So then after the Lord had spoken unto them, he was received up into heaven, and sat on the right hand of God."* Mark 16:19

> *"But this man, after he had offered one sacrifice for sins for ever, sat down on the right hand of God;"* Hebrews 10:12

As stated previously, the theme we have chosen for the book of Hebrews is "Christ is Superior." In verses 2 and 3, we saw seven ways that the Son Jesus Christ is unique in nature, title, and function. We will now see seven Old Testament references as to how Christ is superior to angels. God at sundry times had messengers; now His final message comes from Someone infinitely superior. Nearly every commentator consulted referred to the insertion of this pericope (section) as abrupt and sought to explain the author's reasoning. They said much about the exalted position that angels held in the minds of 1st century Jewish people. Though this writer takes for granted that they are correct, we need not spend much time worrying about such things as we know that it was the Holy Spirit Who inspired the writing, and its place is right where *He* wants it. The idea that we cannot properly exegete scripture until we understand the 'world behind the text' has at least two problems: (1) it often puts scholarship in the way of the Holy Spirit's enlightenment of the text, and (2) it limits the text to only that which the human author meant and understood. In both cases, the issue is that the Holy Spirit's work *began* with the inspiration of the original documents ("For the prophecy came not in old time by the will of man: but holy men of God spake *as they were* moved by the Holy Ghost." II Peter 1:21) and continues through preservation (*"The words of the LORD are pure words: as silver tried in a furnace of earth, purified seven times. Thou shalt keep them, O LORD, thou shalt preserve them from this generation for ever."* Psalms 12:6,7), and to the mind of its modern-day reader (*"But there is a spirit in man: and the inspiration of the Almighty giveth them understanding."* Job 32:8 and *"All scripture is given by inspiration of God, and is profitable for doctrine, for reproof, for correction, for instruction in righteousness:"* II Timothy 3:16). The point is that far too much ink has been spilt trying to explain what the human author's intentions were. Many times, the human authors did not even understand what they were writing (for an example, see Daniel 12:8,9).

The reason for pointing out the sevenfold structures within this first chapter is that the number "7" holds a very special place within the pages of scripture. Arranging things in a sevenfold pattern appears to be a signature that God builds into His works, including Scripture. It has been given a connotation of 'completion' or 'perfection.' This is important because we have been discussing God's final revelation in the Person of His Son, the Author and Finisher of our faith (Hebrews 12:2).

God created the world in one week of seven days.

Christ's redemptive work was accomplished over 1 week.

The Passover that prefigured it took a week of seven days.

There are a total of seven resurrections referred to in Scripture.

The Psalm cited above (Psalm 12:6.7) says that God's words have been purified seven times.

There are seven churches in Revelation, seven trumpets, seven seals, etc.

Sevens even occur in multiples of seven, 'seven' occurring 287 times (7 x 41), 'Seventh' occurring 98 times (7 x 14), 'sevenfold' occurring 7 times, etc., etc., etc.

For our purposes, there are the two sevens we mentioned in the first chapter of Hebrews, plus seven "better" things in Hebrews (a better testament in 7:22, better promises in 8:6, better substance in 10:34, etc., seven titles of Christ in Hebrews, seven 'once's, and seven exhortations.

It is also of interest that the Hebrew word for 'seven' (שֶׁבַע) has the meaning of cessation or rest. This is probably because on the seventh day of creation God rested. It forms the root for 'sabbath,' the day God gave for the people of Israel to rest. This is mentioned because 'rest' is a major theme in chapters 3 and 4 of Hebrews.[29]

> *"Being made so much better than the angels, as he hath by inheritance obtained a more excellent name than they."* v. 4

The phrase *"being made"* occurs in 1:4 here and again in 5:9 and has been viewed as an open door for many heretical commentators to march confidently through, however it isn't hard to understand what is happening in both places. Christ was God outside of time, then stepped into time to accomplish the Father's will. His essential

---

[29] Much of the information in this section is taken from Bullinger's *Numbers In Scripture*, Kregel Publications.

nature does not change (He is always God), but His 'status' does temporarily. He isn't 'made', He voluntarily sets aside His glory and privilege to accomplish redemption. Chapter 2 speaks of Christ being "a little lower than the angels". This is the same sense. He is God, but He became man, a 'lower' order of being than angels for the purposes of salvation; He isn't a lower Being in an essential sense.[30]

His 'name' becoming more excellent is a brief description of what His name entails now that He is glorified. Believing the Gospel is placing our trust in the death, burial, and resurrection of Christ. It is believing in what He accomplished for our salvation. This is the same as believing on His name, and the Bible uses this phrase in precisely that sense. The name of Christ is shorthand for the work He accomplished for salvation, as He alone bears that distinction.

Christ's inheritance has been addressed previously.

What follows is the seven-fold proof of Christ's superiority, using seven Old Testament references. These references are, in order: (1) Psalm 2:7, (2) II Samuel 7:14, (3) Deuteronomy

---

[30] The 'Prince of Puritans' John Owen organized these ideas by separating Christ's appellations in Scripture as either 'economic', (referring only to Christ's redemptive function), or 'ontological' (referring to His true essential nature as a Person in the Trinity, i.e., God). This distinction may be helpful to some.

32:43, (4) Psalm 104:4, (5) Psalm 45:6-7, (6) Psalm 102:25-27, and (7) Psalm 110:1.

> *"For unto which of the angels said he at any time, Thou art my Son, this day have I begotten thee? And again, I will be to him a Father, and he shall be to me a Son?"* v. 5

Verse 5 contains the first two references. The first is from Psalm 2:7, the second from II Samuel 7:14 (or I Chronicles 17:13).

> *"And again, when he bringeth in the firstbegotten into the world, he saith, And let all the angels of God worship him."* v. 6

This is from Deuteronomy 32:43. Adam was 'the son of God' (Luke 3:38), but only Christ was begotten by Him. 'Firstbegotten' has the same sense as Christ being the 'firstfruits of the resurrection' in I Corinthians 15:20. Everyone else's resurrection is requisite upon Christ's resurrection, so everyone else that is 'begotten of God (saved, born again),' the two ideas being combined in I Peter 1:3.

> *"And of the angels he saith, Who maketh his angels spirits, and his ministers a flame of fire."* v. 7

This is from Psalm 104:4.

> *"But unto the Son he saith, Thy throne, O God, is for ever and ever: a sceptre of righteousness is the sceptre of thy kingdom. Thou hast loved righteousness, and hated iniquity; therefore God, even thy*

God, hath anointed thee with the oil of gladness above thy fellows." v. 8,9

Psalm 45:6,7. We agree with Oliver B. Greene's comments concerning the Kingly anointing that was prefigured by the previous occupants of the throne of David.[31] This agrees with and unifies both contexts (O.T. and N.T.).

"And, Thou, Lord, in the beginning hast laid the foundation of the earth; and the heavens are the works of thine hands: They shall perish; but thou remainest; and they all shall wax old as doth a garment; And as a vesture shalt thou fold them up, and they shall be changed: but thou art the same, and thy years shall not fail."

Psalm 102:25-27. The final phrases of the verse hold special meaning for quantum theorists who posit how extra dimensions may be arranged. We await the answers of the Weaver of the vesture, Who doesn't exist in another dimension, but is altogether outside them all.

"But to which of the angels said he at any time, Sit on my right hand, until I make thine enemies thy footstool?" v. 13

Psalm 110:1. We would only add I Corinthians 15:26.

"The last enemy that shall be destroyed is death."

---

[31] Greene, Oliver B., *The Epistle of Paul the Apostle to the Hebrews* (Gospel Hour, Inc. 1965), p. 42.

> *"Are they not all ministering spirits, sent forth to minister for them who shall be heirs of salvation?"* v. 14

This is not an Old Testament quotation, but rather a statement. There is far too much speculation concerning what function angels currently play. We should be satisfied with what the Bible says directly. Some words of warning are also in order, and they come from the Apostle Paul:

> *"And no marvel; for Satan himself is transformed into an angel of light."*

II Corinthians 11:14.

> *"But though we, or an angel from heaven, preach any other gospel unto you than that which we have preached unto you, let him be accursed."* Galatians 1:8.

As has been stated, Christ is God's final revelation. All other 'messengers' must have their messages weighed against God's word. Paul even warned of the possibility of the Apostles themselves being fallible. The verse says that angels are sent forth to minister to those who will become the heirs of salvation. This doesn't include adding anything to the Bible or the Gospel. It is interesting that many false religions are started when a man gets a vision of an angelic apparition. These include, but are not limited to: Mormonism,[32] Scientology, and Islam[33]. The

---

[32] ChurchofJesusChrist.org. https://www.churchofjesuschrist.org/study/history/topics/angel-moroni?lang=eng.

[33] Encyclopedia Britannica "Quran." Qur'an | Description, Meaning, History, & Facts | Britannica.

Jehovah's Witnesses claim that Michael the archangel *is* Jesus.[34] Does the text we are considering leave any room for this conclusion?

Much, much more about angels could be presented here, but it lies outside of the parameters of our theme of Christ's superiority. As a review, there are seven aspects of His superiority to angels.

(1) He is the Son of God (v. 5a).
(2) He is the promised Son of David and Inheritor of His throne (v. 5b).
(3) He is the Supreme Authority of Whom the angels worship as God (v. 6).
(4) His ministry is eternal, unlike that of the angels (v. 7).
(5) His ministry is that of Ruler and King (vv. 8,9).
(6) He is the immutable Creator (vv. 10-12).
(7) He is the Sovereign Ruler and Victor over all His enemies (v. 13).

---

[34] JW.org. https://www.jw.org/en /bible-teachings/questions/archangel-michael/.

HEBREWS CHAPTER 2

"I hate change! It's too disruptive! When things are different, you have to think about the change and deal with it! I like things to stay the same, so I can take everything for granted!"- Calvin[35]

As we head into the second chapter of this book, we shift literary genre slightly. It was mentioned before that there are 5 warning passages in the book of Hebrews, and this is the first of these. They are like parentheses where the author stops momentarily to exhort his audience based on his line of reasoning to that point. We believe it will benefit us to understand where these are, why they are there, and what they mean for us. To that end, we offer this chart, adapted from Dr. Thomas Constable:[36]

Doctrinal treatise	Warning passage
Chapter 1	2:1-4
2:5-18	3:1-4:14
4:15-5:10	5:11-6:12
6:13-10:18	10:19-39
Chapter 11	Chapters 12-13

---

[35] Watterson, Bill *There's Treasure Everywhere* (Andrews and McMeel, 1996), p. 72.
[36] Constable, *Hebrews*, p. 7.

Why this is so important is that the author meant to exhort the immediate readers toward Christ. Their unique circumstances caused the author to put a sharp edge on the warnings and to use modes of speech that can be misinterpreted if the context is misunderstood. To avoid this, we will remind ourselves of the context as we go along, as well as keeping 'Christ is superior' at the front of our minds.

> *"Therefore we ought to give the more earnest heed to the things which we have heard, lest at any time we should let them slip."* Hebrews 2:1

There is a well-worn axiom in fundamental theology: "When you see a 'therefore', stop and see what it's there for."

This is the reason for the short review above. The revelation of Christ deserves more earnest heed because of the understanding that it was so far superior to what had come before.

> *"For if the word spoken by angels was stedfast, and every transgression and disobedience received a just recompence of reward; How shall we escape, if we neglect so great salvation; which at the first began to be spoken by the Lord, and was confirmed unto us by them that heard him;"* vv. 2-3

What is the writer talking about here, specifically?! Take a look at Galatians 3:19.

> *"Wherefore then serveth the law? It was added because of transgressions, till*

*the seed should come to whom the promise
was made; and it was ordained by angels in
the hand of a mediator."*

Now look at Acts 7:48-53.

*"Howbeit the most High dwelleth not
in temples made with hands; as saith the
prophet, Heaven is my throne, and earth is
my footstool: what house will ye build me?
saith the Lord: or what is the place of my
rest? Hath not my hand made all these
things? Ye stiffnecked and uncircumcised in
heart and ears, ye do always resist the Holy
Ghost: as your fathers did, so do ye. Which
of the prophets have not your fathers
persecuted? and they have slain them which
shewed before of the coming of the Just
One; of whom ye have been now the
betrayers and murderers: Who have
received the law by the disposition of angels,
and have not kept it."*

These verses say that the law was
administered from God, by angels, to man. Now
let's see how 'the fathers' honored that revelation.
Go to Acts 7:38.

*"This is he, that was in the church in
the wilderness with the angel which spake to
him in the mount Sina, and with our fathers:
who received the lively oracles to give unto
us:"*

The stick picker-upper was stoned. Miriam was judged with leprosy. The sons of Korah were swallowed up.

Is this the point of the current exhortation? Is this what the author's warning was about? Who gets stoned nowadays? Who gets stricken with leprosy for disobeying God? When is the last time you saw the Earth swallow up people for challenging the preacher?

In verse 1, the author uses the pronoun "we." This does not mean "us Jews." This book isn't written to Jewish people in general, it is written to Jewish Christians. Now let's ask a few questions.

(1) Is there any difference between those Christians and us today regarding the mode and benefits of salvation?
(2) Did they have eternal security as we do today?
(3) If so, they cannot lose their salvation. They are in Christ just as we. What then do they stand in danger of? What can be lost?
(4) What salvation is here being spoken of?

To answer these questions, we should carry the type out to its conclusion. The escape of the children of Israel from Egypt represents salvation. The blood of the Passover lamb was shed, separating the living from the dead. To Egypt, a type of the world, Israel was a thorn in the flesh, and they were glad to see them go. The only one upset about losing them was Pharaoh, who typifies the devil, the god of this world who sent his demon hordes (Pharaoh's army) to harry them. They go 3 days' journey into the wilderness where they cross the Red Sea. This is a picture of your spiritual baptism. It brought protection from the Egyptian army's trying to repossess them and should have guaranteed their entrance into an abundant Christian life (or the enjoyment of the Promised Land). This, however, was not the case. The first generation that left Egypt did not get something they had been promised despite leaving Egypt, despite going through the Sea, despite being circumcised. They languished in the wilderness for the rest of their lives. What did they miss out on? Their inheritance! Three sons of Jacob also lost part of their inheritance: Reuben, Simeon, and Levi. Esau lost his inheritance, and there are things we can lose!

We, just as they, can lose something that the Bible promises: Part of our inheritance. We will absolutely escape condemnation. We will receive eternal life. We will either be raptured or resurrected, and we will be glorified. This is salvation *neglected*, not salvation *rejected*. What then does a Christian stand to lose? Things like the crown of life (James 1:12, Revelation 2:10), praise from God (Matthew 25:21, 23; Luke 19:17, 19; II Timothy 4:8, etc.), rewards (I Corinthians 3:8, Colossians 3:24, Revelation 2:7, etc.).

These are all future things that can be affected by our current faithfulness; but to understand fully what this passage is getting at, we need to go just a bit further. One of the best ways to illustrate the fulness of our salvation and to help understand tricky passages like this one is to view our salvation as happening in three tenses.[37]

(1) **Past**-you have been saved. You were put 'in Christ'.
(2) **Present**-you are being saved from sin's power.
(3) **Future**-you will be saved from death and Hell, and resurrected, or raptured, and glorified.

It is this present aspect that we believe the author is trying to put across. Our present 'salvation' is something that is voluntarily participated in. In other words, God has offered you a way to triumph over sin's power in your life, but you must take advantage. James 4:7 says *"Submit yourselves therefore to God. Resist the devil, and he will flee from you."* Sin has consequences, and if we fail to avail ourselves of the power that is offered through ministry of the Holy Spirit, we expose ourselves to those consequences. Check out I Corinthians 10:1-13.

> *"Moreover, brethren, I would not that ye should be ignorant, how that all our fathers were under the cloud, and all passed through the sea; And were all baptized unto Moses in the cloud and in the sea; And did all eat the same spiritual meat; And did all drink the same spiritual drink: for they drank of that spiritual Rock that followed them: and*

---

[37] See Rokser, Dennis M., *Salvation in Three Time Zones* (Grace Gospel Press, 2013).

that Rock was Christ. But with many of them God was not well pleased: for they were overthrown in the wilderness. Now these things were our examples, to the intent we should not lust after evil things, as they also lusted. Neither be ye idolaters, as were some of them; as it is written, The people sat down to eat and drink, and rose up to play. Neither let us commit fornication, as some of them committed, and fell in one day three and twenty thousand. Neither let us tempt Christ, as some of them also tempted, and were destroyed of serpents. Neither murmur ye, as some of them also murmured, and were destroyed of the destroyer. Now all these things happened unto them for ensamples: and they are written for our admonition, upon whom the ends of the world are come. Wherefore let him that thinketh he standeth take heed lest he fall. There hath no temptation taken you but such as is common to man: but God is faithful, who will not suffer you to be tempted above that ye are able; but will with the temptation also make a way to escape, that ye may be able to bear it."

For the original readers of Hebrews, their failure to 'give the more earnest heed' would have dire consequences. As stated previously in these lessons, the Roman emperor Titus would besiege Jerusalem shortly after this letter was written. We don't know if anyone ignored this letter and returned to Jerusalem, but if they did, they saw horrific destruction and probably lost their lives in a violent way.

We have a similar warning, but our outcome is somewhat different. It is tragic, nonetheless. Our version of failure to give heed can result in:

(1) The short-term consequences of our actions.
(2) The long-term effects of our non-Biblical lifestyle.
(3) A failure to produce fruit in our own lives (the fruit of the Spirit Gal. 5:22).
(4) The failure to produce fruit in others (sharing the Gospel, discipleship, testimony).
(5) The loss of the things mentioned above (crowns, rewards, reigning, praise of God, etc.).

"God also bearing them witness, both with signs and wonders, and with divers miracles, and gifts of the Holy Ghost, according to his own will?" v. 4

God blessed the revelation of Christ and confirmed it with signs, wonders, miracles, and gifts of the Holy Ghost. These are found throughout the book of Acts. These were a signal-a HUGE flashing light-to those who heard of the salvation "which at the first began to be spoken by the Lord." This is the revelation we have been talking about. Christ as superior. It was inaugurated by signs and wonders because something had changed in God's program of the ages or dispensations. Let us ask you this: What revelation is the current 'signs and wonders' movement heralding? Remember: Christ is the final revelation concerning God. His salvation is final.

> *"For unto the angels hath he not put in subjection the world to come, whereof we speak."* v. 5

The return to the idea of the angels, plus the reference to what has been said ("whereof we speak") not only supports the idea that 2:1-4 was a parenthesis, it indicates a return to the exposition that began with chapter 1.

"The world to come" refers to the Millennial Reign of Christ, where Christ will physically, literally reign on Earth from Jerusalem, in fulfillment of the Abrahamic, Davidic, and New Covenants, as well as all the Messianic prophecies of the Old Testament.

This reign *will* happen, and it *will not* be administered by angels.

> "It is hard to imagine how replacement theologians can ignore a literal millennial period of reign by Messiah, but they do. However, the author of Hebrews is addressing a Jewish audience who were (and who are) expecting a dispensation where Messiah will rule on earth. They expect this because this is what their Scriptures proclaim, and it is what the author of Hebrews clearly indicates is coming. Don't be misled into accepting the idea that the

church has replaced Israel. The Bible never proclaims this, in either testament."[38]

"But one in a certain place testified, saying, What is man, that thou art mindful of him? or the son of man, that thou visitest him? Thou madest him a little lower than the angels; thou crownedst him with glory and honour, and didst set him over the works of thy hands: Thou hast put all things in subjection under his feet." vv. 6-8a

This is a quotation from Psalm 8:4-6. The author takes for granted that his readers or hearers would immediately recognize this as such. Not only is this a part of the Tanakh, or Hebrew Bible (our Old Testament) in which every Jewish person was well versed, but it was also a song sung by Israel choirs for the preceding 1,000 years.

Looking at the world around him, David was blown away that God would create everything that He did, and then place someone as fickle as man over it. That the Creator of the Universe would pay any attention at all to man was even more astonishing. Even the greatest of men are often a disappointment. Christian, take comfort. The fact that God is infinite means that He can care for you personally; as the song says, "He Loves Me Like I Was His Only Child." Along with the rest of us, you

---

[38] Emlen, S., "Charlie" Garret and Voitenko, Sergio *Hebrews* (from SuperiorWord.org, https://study-pdfs.s3.amazonaws.com/hebrews-commentary-rev2.pdf, 2022), p. 40.

can be amazed that He would, but you should enjoy the fact that He does.

We agree with most writers on the meaning of this passage, which is that it is a reference to mankind in general, not specifically the Messiah.[39] We're not saying that there isn't a Messianic fulfillment in Psalm 8, we believe there is,[40] but the writer to the Hebrews uses it the way David probably meant it, which is that David is pondering man as a creation of God.

The reason we prefer this view is that (1) the passage doesn't make nearly as much sense if referring to only Christ, (2) doing so would make verse 9 redundant, and (3) using the text in this way (mankind in general) brings to the fore the breathtakingly glorious spiritual truth that we think the author was getting at. The things listed here (made a little lower than the angels, crowned with glory and honor, and dominion) were all bestowed upon Adam at the original Creation, but he failed in fulfilling God's purpose in bestowing them when

---

[39] Barclay, *Hebrews*, p 15.

[40] There are many instances where a passage refers to two different people or things. A passage in Ezekiel 28 refers directly to the king of Tyre but includes details that can only metaphorically applied to him. These details can be directly applied to Satan, while the others are metaphorical to him. The line between the two is blurred and is a testament to the Holy Spirit's skill as a poet and wordsmith. A second passage occurs in Job 41 where, again, we have details that can refer only directly to a plesiosaurian sea monster, and metaphorically to Satan, and vice versa. This idea is known in hermeneutics as the rule of 'Double reference.' Psalm 22 is also a great example.

he fell into sin. Jesus Christ, the 'second man' and 'last Adam' (I Corinthians 15:45, 47), was also 'made a little lower than the angels' (v. 9) and by His perfect life and work, sinless death and glorious resurrection won mankind's right to glory, honor, and dominion, and will ultimately fulfill God's purposes!

> *"That the God of our Lord Jesus Christ, the Father of glory, may give unto you the spirit of wisdom and revelation in the knowledge of him: The eyes of your understanding being enlightened; that ye may know what is the hope of his calling, and what the riches of the glory of his inheritance in the saints, And what is the exceeding greatness of his power to us-ward who believe, according to the working of his mighty power, Which he wrought in Christ, when he raised him from the dead, and set him at his own right hand in the heavenly places, Far above all principality, and power, and might, and dominion, and every name that is named, not only in this world, but also in that which is to come: And hath put all things under his feet, and gave him to be the head over all things to the church, Which is his body, the fulness of him that filleth all in all."* Ephesians 1:17-23

> *"For in that he put all in subjection under him, he left nothing that is not put under him. But now we see not yet all things put under him."* v. 8b

This portion is separated from the rest because it goes beyond the Psalmist's citation. This was God's purpose in man. Man had dominion and was subject only to God. He was not even subject to death, until death came with the Fall. However, there is a beautiful, wonderful word inserted here. That word is 'yet'. Jesus Christ will fulfill God's purpose and put all things under Himself, including death. This fact makes Satan's offer in Matthew 4:8 and 9 meaningless:

> *"Again, the devil taketh him up into an exceeding high mountain, and sheweth him all the kingdoms of the world, and the glory of them; And saith unto him, All these things will I give thee, if thou wilt fall down and worship me."*

As always, Christ had the perfect answer in verse 10: *"Get thee hence, Satan: for it is written, Thou shalt worship the Lord thy God, and him only shalt thou serve."* Jesus Christ will receive that worship from every creature-either willingly or unwillingly-in the day when He puts all things under His feet. Perhaps the angels recognized the profound implications of such a reply for in the next verse they "came and ministered unto him." (Reminds one of Hebrews 1:14...are they not all ministers?)

But it gets even better. Check out II Timothy 2:12:

> *"If we suffer, we shall also reign with him: if we deny him, he also will deny us:"*

Also, Revelation 5:8-10:

"And when he had taken the book, the four beasts and four and twenty elders fell down before the Lamb, having every one of them harps, and golden vials full of odours, which are the prayers of saints. And they sung a new song, saying, Thou art worthy to take the book, and to open the seals thereof: for thou wast slain, and hast redeemed us to God by thy blood out of every kindred, and tongue, and people, and nation; And hast made us unto our God kings and priests: and we shall reign on the earth."

And finally, Revelation 20:4-6:

"And I saw thrones, and they sat upon them, and judgment was given unto them: and I saw the souls of them that were beheaded for the witness of Jesus, and for the word of God, and which had not worshipped the beast, neither his image, neither had received his mark upon their foreheads, or in their hands; and they lived and reigned with Christ a thousand years. But the rest of the dead lived not again until the thousand years were finished. This is the first resurrection. Blessed and holy is he that hath part in the first resurrection: on such the second death hath no power, but they shall be priests of God and of Christ, and shall reign with him a thousand years."

You see, there is coming a day that man *will* fulfill his destiny. Because Christ won back man's right to reign, when He reigns for a thousand years, we will also reign with Him!

> *"But we see Jesus, who was made a little lower than the angels for the suffering of death, crowned with glory and honour; that he by the grace of God should taste death for every man."* v. 9

And there it is. *"But we see Jesus"*! Man sinned, *"But we see Jesus."* It looked like Satan won, *"But we see Jesus."* Death seemed like the final word, *"But we see Jesus!"*

In *"being made a little lower than the angels,"* Christ took on humanity *"for the suffering of death."* His death was planned from eternity past because God knew how it was going to go down. Though He didn't cause Adam to sin, He knew he would.

> "It was impossible that Deity should die. If He would taste death for every man, He must become Man, for only as a man could He die."[41]

> "...Christ undertook a work which was far above the power of all the angels, and yet to effect it He was made lower than them! If ever power was made perfect in weakness, it was in this!"[42]

---

[41] Ironside, *Hebrews and Titus*, p. 45.

[42] Pink, Arthur W., *An Exposition of Hebrews* (Baker Book House, 1974), pp. 107-8.

Devotionally, we are to take the example of Christ's humiliation and apply it directly to ourselves. If you are a Christian, you are meant to be a servant. You may not have known it, but it's part of the deal.

Have you ever been close enough to a grown man's feet to analyze the aromatic palette? It's not pretty! Yet the God of the universe-the Holy One, the One from Whose presence the earth and heaven flee away, the sinless One, not only became Man and walked on Earth, but put up with people for 33 years. He stooped down and lovingly washed the feet of those whose every sin and wayward thought He knew in vivid color...

Christ was crowned with glory as a result of faithfully executing His work. Our reign with Him as mentioned above is in direct relation to our faithful service. This is why Jesus says, *"But many that are first shall be last; and the last shall be first."* (Matthew 19:30, Mark 10:31) and "If any man desire to be first, *the same* shall be last of all, and servant of all." Mark 9:35.

Christ was crowned with the glory and honor that man lost, and He tasted death for <u>every man</u>. There isn't any way to spin this verse. In fact, with the exception of Darby,[43] there isn't a serious

---

[43] John Nelson Darby changed the reading from *everyone* or *every man*, to *everything*. Christ's death was to pay for the sin of mankind. 'Everything' did not sin though all Creation was affected. Christ's resurrection guarantees the redemption and restoration of Creation. Christ appeared as a man, and it is to men that He came to be accepted. If he wanted to regenerate fallen sea cucumbers, He would have come as a sea cucumber.

translation out there that has the audacity to change it. Christ died for EVERY MAN! There isn't a man (or woman- 'man' is mankind) on the face of the Earth or in all of history that Christ did not die for. It was an unlimited atonement, free to all! This is one of the clearest statements in all of Scripture contradicting the idea that Christ's death was for a select few only.

Before we get back into the text, let's be sure to stress again that the reason this passage (2:5-3:6) is here has everything to do with what the author's audience faced on a regular basis. They had faithful disciples preaching Christ in one ear, and blind Jews filling the other ear with Christ's death as a defeat. They might say, "How could this be God's plan? Things didn't happen the way they were supposed to!"

Abrahamic (as opposed to Messianic) Jewish people had some issues when it came to accepting Christ. The first is found in Numbers 23:19: *"God is not a man, that he should lie; neither the son of man, that he should repent: hath he said, and shall he not do it? or hath he spoken, and shall he not make it good?"* God was God, and man was man. God was holy and utterly separate. Of course, this verse is referring to a facet of God's character, and not His essence, for when He became a man-or better, *put on* humanity-these aspects did not change.

Another problem had to do with His Messianic claims. Their Messiah was supposed to sweep in, relieve Israel of their oppressors and reign over an epoch of great prosperity; not suffer and die. These things would be the go-to arguments for

Abrahamic Jews arguing against these Jewish Christians. This would be very discouraging to them; therefore, the author of Hebrews is at great pains to elucidate just why God did what He did in His incarnation and passion.

> *"For it became him, for whom are all things, and by whom are all things, in bringing many sons unto glory, to make the captain of their salvation perfect through sufferings."* v. 10

"For it became him," It did not make sense to some why Christ would come, with all Israel's national hopes bound up in him, only to die at the hands of Gentile pagans, and at the behest of His treacherous brethren. If He is Ha Mashiach, the Messiah, this is beneath Him! Alexander Maclaren has a good quote here for them and for us:

> "It does not 'become' us to be hasty or confident in determining what 'becomes' God…Perhaps we have not quite got to the bottom of the bottomless;"[44]

It is God's prerogative to act as He pleases, with or without our knowledge. In Luke 24:25-26 Jesus says: *"O fools, and slow of heart to believe all that the prophets have spoken: Ought not Christ to have suffered these things, and to enter into his glory?"* The preaching in the book of Acts followed similarly:

---

[44] MacLaren, Alexander, *Expositions of Holy Scripture, Vol. 10* (Eerdmans, 1952), p. 228.

"Ye men of Israel, hear these words; Jesus of Nazareth, a man approved of God among you by miracles and wonders and signs, which God did by him in the midst of you, as ye yourselves also know: Him, being delivered by the determinate counsel and foreknowledge of God, ye have taken, and by wicked hands have crucified and slain: Whom God hath raised up, having loosed the pains of death: because it was not possible that he should be holden of it." Acts 2:22-24

The way this verse reads is wonderful because it illustrates perfectly how divine foreknowledge works. Jesus preached the 'gospel of the kingdom' to Israel. They, of their own free will, rejected it and put Christ to death. Yet everything happened according to God's 'determinate counsel and foreknowledge.' The fact that God knew what they were going to do did not negate their freedom in choosing. The Jewish religious leadership delivered Christ up to the Romans for execution, but somehow it was also the will of God that He should die. The offer of the kingdom was real, yet God knew they would refuse it. This led to the temporary setting aside of Israel and the coming in of church age. The world was blessed by Israel's rejection of her King, as the Gospel went into all the world, but it will be blessed even more one day when she accepts Him!

"For if the casting away of them be the reconciling of the world, what shall the

receiving of them be, but life from the dead?"
Romans 11:15.

The way God has planned and crafted the ages far exceeds anything man has ever contrived or conceived. It is beautiful and wonderful, and He has covered every base. It is we who wander around haplessly and ignorantly, ever critical of how God is handling things.

Just for fun, here are a couple hints that God built into the Jews' own Holy Book, the Tanakh-our Old Testament-that told them the fruit of acceptance and rejection. In other words, they may not have seen it, but it was there all along:

Abel was killed by his brother Cain. Abel's sacrifice was acceptable to God. The book of Hebrews compares Christ with Abel in Chapter 12.

Joseph is one of the great types of Christ in the Old Testament. He was delivered by his brethren out of jealousy. They suffer while he is away, but eventually he reveals himself to them and they go to live with him and enjoy the blessings of his earthly reign in Egypt which is a type of the world.

Christ even told the religious hierarchy of His time what they would do in the vineyard parable of Matthew 21, and they did it. They slew the Son of the vineyard Owner. Did they all participate? No. Nicodemus, for one, did not. He chose not to. We quoted a verse from Romans 11 above. The context of that chapter is God's dealing with His people, the Jews. An 'elect' remnant were saved, and the rest were blinded. The remnant is not individuals, but a group, as are the 'blinded'. We have the God-given ability and opportunity to decide which group we are in. Some will be blinded; some will be saved. God will do it. His will absolutely will be done. You'd better get on the right side of it.

> *"for whom are all things, and by whom*
> *are all things,"*

Every commentator reviewed said that this is a reference to God the Father. We would like to point out that while *"In the beginning God created the heaven and the earth,"* the *"for whom"* and *"by whom"* have more direct cross-reference to Christ in Colossians 1:16. Christ was the agent of creation and the One for Whose pleasure it was created. He is both the benefactor and the beneficiary. So, Who is the 'Whom' referred to here, God the Father, or God the Son? The answer is "yes".

> *"in bringing many sons unto glory"*

Despite what we saw previously-that Christ's death was for 'every man' (every member of mankind)-this phrase causes the hyper-Calvinist to salivate. Many is less than all! See? See? It is only 'sons' that are brought to glory! The emphasis here is not on salvation generally, but on glorification specifically. Do you remember the three tenses of salvation? 'Glory' isn't the first one, it is the last one. You must be a son before you can be brought to glory! The idea being stressed is also that of many in opposition to few. The author shows how effective the plan was. Christ's death would not save a few, but very many! Now, hold onto that while we get the next phrase:

> *"to make the captain of their salvation
> perfect through sufferings"*

Here is this passage paraphrased: "God saw fit that in performing the great work of securing the glorification of those that will be saved, that suffering should be the road their prototype should take." 'Prototype' may not be the best term to use, but here is why it was selected: the text calls Christ the 'captain' of our salvation. The Greek word behind the English one is translated other ways in other places, but we miss some really cool stuff when we ignore the majesty of the King's English to try and find clarity in a language no one here understands.

When this writer was in high school, we had a basketball team. Our team had a team captain. This person exhibited leadership but was also a participant in the game.[45]

This writer realizes that none of the translators 400 years ago had his basketball team in view. The point is that the team captain didn't order the teammates around from off the court. He was a player who led the way by being a player himself and playing the game how it ought to be played. Christ didn't just tell us to 'take up our cross' (Matthew 16:24); He physically, literally took up His. He 'blazed the trail' He wanted His followers to take. Let's look at a few more reasons why the second Westminster Company might have selected the term 'captain'.

---

[45] See also Arthur W. Pink's treatment of 'captain' in *Hebrews*, p. 156.

"A captain in the period prior to the professionalization of the armed services of European nations subsequent to the <u>French Revolution</u>, during the <u>early modern period</u>, was a nobleman who purchased the right to head a company from the previous holder of that right. He would in turn receive money from another nobleman to serve as his <u>lieutenant</u>. The funding to provide for the troops did not come from the monarch or their government; the captain was responsible for feeding, housing, and provisioning their company. If he was unable to support the company, or was otherwise court-martialed, he would be dismissed ("<u>cashiered</u>"), and the monarch would sell his commission to another nobleman to command the company."[46]

Christ 'purchased' the right to lead His company (believers) on the cross. It is His responsibility to make provision for us. He doesn't just send us a check. He is in the boat with us, so no matter what the conditions are on the sea of life, our Captain is with us, and we will be saved in proportion to His ability to fulfill His responsibilities.

"make…perfect through sufferings"

One says, "So you're saying Christ had to be 'made' perfect? I thought He was *already* perfect." Pink answers: "The reference is not to the person

---

[46]This quotation was taken directly from Wikipedia's article on the term 'captain'. Captain (armed forces) - Wikipedia. Accessed 5/12/23.

of Christ, but to a particular office which He fills."[47] Christ was indeed perfect in character. His impeccability is established. Suffering wouldn't make someone perfect in character (this sounds like penance!). No, this is saying Christ is fit for the title 'Captain of salvation' by participating in suffering, as we have been discussing. Please bear in mind that His suffering was different than ours is, but we follow His example, nonetheless. None of what we know as Christians, from our deliverance from sin and death to the blessings of our life and calling, to the glory that lies ahead would be possible without His great work of death on the cross. We don't bear His cross to win salvation, He did that for us. We bear His cross for the sake of others, just as He did.

> "The idea of being "made perfect" is tied directly to the words of verse 7 where it says, "You have crowned him with glory and honor." This making perfect does not carry the idea of being made "better," as if there was a lack in Christ. Rather, it speaks of bringing to completion, or meeting, the goal. Christ suffered, was crucified, and died with the intent of bringing God's plan of salvation to fruition."[48]

Let's zoom back out to get the lesson here. As stated above, an unexpected, violent death is not typically the best way to set forth the superiority of a hero. The recipients of the letter to

---

[47] Pink, *Hebrews*, p. 157.
[48] Garrett & Voitenko, *Hebrews*, p. 50.

the Hebrews needed to see that Christ's suffering and death was merely a stage in the process of ultimate glory. Christ won a title He otherwise wouldn't have had a right to because of the nature of Divine justice. God must judge sin because of His holy character. He often withholds His judgment out of mercy (Habakkuk 1:13), but He will judge it. Your sin will be paid for. If you accept the suffering and death of Christ for your sin, you may take advantage of His payment on your behalf. If you do not, you will pay for it yourself.

Sin is by nature transgression against God. Since God is an infinite Being, there is an infinite depth to the transgression. Only a sacrifice of an infinite nature could accomplish satisfaction for the crime. Because of this, Christ is uniquely qualified for such a death. Even in His most ignominious act, Christ proves Himself superior to every other being in the universe.

> *"For it became him, ... to make the captain of their salvation perfect through sufferings. For both he that sanctifieth and they who are sanctified are all of one: for which cause he is not ashamed to call them brethren,"* vv. 10-11

Verse 11 does not stand alone, as the word "for" connects the preceding verse to it. There is a profound truth that unfolds beautifully when these verses, taken together, are properly understood.

We saw how the Captain led the way, not by simply telling us what to do or how to live, but by living out the example for all to see. This is one of the major reasons for the Gospel accounts. When we see Luke telling us that Christ was *"led by the Spirit into the wilderness"* in 4:1, it cannot be because He didn't know where to go. He is demonstrating the Spirit-led life. When we hear Him praying to His Father, it is not to inform God of something, or to get an answer from Him, they are both omniscient! He is living out the ideal prayer life for all to see. When he prays: *"O my Father, if it be possible, let this cup pass from me: nevertheless not as I will, but as thou wilt."* (Matt. 26:39), He is not trying to get out of going to the cross, He is living out the consecrated life, the yielded life, as well as reminding us that the cross is the ONLY way our sins could be dealt with.

The profound truth of these verses has to do with what is known as the 'Crucified life.'[49] The Jewish Christians whom the writer is addressing must see God's plan in a Messiah that would suffer and die, instead of conquer and reign. An Isaiah 53 Messiah would come before a Psalm 24 Messiah could. If they were to follow Christ (and we as well), we must follow Him in the path of the cross. Jesus suffered and died for the sake of others. It was God's plan in Christ that we, the 'sons (and daughters) brought to glory,' should be willing to suffer, and if need be, give our lives for others as well.

---

[49] An excellent resource is the book by L.E. Maxwell entitled *Born Crucified*.

The forms of the word 'sanctify' in verse 11 have to do with consecration, and not purification.[50] William Newell says,

> "This is a use of the word "sanctify" common in the book of Hebrews. And this passage, it seems to me, allies itself most intimately with the great high-priestly prayer of John 17, where our Lord prayed: "Sanctify them through thy truth: thy word is truth . . . And for their sakes I sanctify myself, that they also might be sanctified through the truth." This verse removes all thoughts of sanctification in the sense of removal of defilement, for Christ had none. . .In this very prayer our Lord is devoting Himself to that *identification with His own*, which would be consummated the next day on the Cross! He set Himself apart unto that death. . ."[51]

Christ was set apart for the 'crucified life' and sets us who are saved apart for the 'crucified life.'[52] Our being brought to glory (from verse 10) is a given. It will happen (Romans 8:30). We are set apart for that as well. This is our position or standing in Christ. *"But as many as received him, to them gave he power to become the sons of God, even to them that believe on his name:"* (John

---

[50] Thomas, W.H. Griffith, *Let Us Go On* (Zondervan, 1944), p. 35.
[51] Newell, William, *Hebrews Verse by Verse* (World Bible Publishers, 1947), p. 52-53.
[52] Gaebelein, *Annotated Bible*, p. 247.

1:12). Our standing in Christ cannot change, and He is not ashamed to call us brethren!

The idea of being *"of one"* simply means that we have the same source, in a sense.[53] The Holy Spirit overshadowed Mary (Luke 1:35), and we are born of the Spirit (John 3:5) as well. We are sons of God; He is *the* Son of God. We are flesh and bone, and He took on flesh and bone to redeem us.

> *"Saying, I will declare thy name unto my brethren, in the midst of the church will I sing praise unto thee. And again, I will put my trust in him. And again, Behold I and the children which God hath given me."* vv. 12-13

What follows are more Old Testament references to bolster the writer's point. The first is from Psalm 22:22, the second from Isaiah 8:18.

> *"Forasmuch then as the children are partakers of flesh and blood, he also himself likewise took part of the same; that through death he might destroy him that had the power of death, that is, the devil;"* v. 14

We see here the necessity of Christ's adding humanity to accomplish salvation for humankind. To redeem men, He must become a man. Alexander Maclaren makes the shocking observation that "His creative agency was not the highest exhibition of His power." Creation was an act of sheer will and was spoken into existence in a word. But the 'bringing of many sons to glory'

---

[53] Wuest, *Hebrews*, p. 61.

took a grueling process of condescension, agony, death, and resurrection.[54] What a monumental work the cross was! As thankful as we are for God's beautiful creation, it pales in comparison to our thankfulness to Him for the cross. Seeing the wrath of God poured out on Him for sin we committed and knowing everything He went through for us is what makes the Christian cringe when someone uses the name of Jesus Christ irreverently...

"Him that hath the power of death" is stated to be the devil. His 'power of death' lies in his ability to draw men and women into sin, for it was that first sin that plunged mankind into death in Genesis 3. God's definition of death is eternal separation from Him in hell, something John called the 'second death' (Rev. 20:14, etc.). A good cross reference for this verse is I John 3:8:

> *"He that committeth sin is of the devil; for the devil sinneth from the beginning. For this purpose the Son of God was manifested, that he might destroy the works of the devil."*

> *"And deliver them who through fear of death were all their lifetime subject to bondage."* v. 15

It is a wonder of salvation that those who have placed their faith in Christ no longer fear death as a proposition. Yes, they may succumb to a fear of the pain and suffering associated with it, but death has become something beautiful-a 'graduation ceremony' of sorts; a cessation of pain

---

[54] Maclaren, *Expositions*, pp.237-8.

and labor, and of entering into the very presence of the One Who bought them. Paul said, *"For to me to live is Christ, and to die is gain."* Philippians 1:21. David said, "In God I will praise his word, in God I have put my trust; I will not fear what flesh can do unto me." Psalm 56:4.

> *"For verily he took not on him the nature of angels; but he took on him the seed of Abraham."* v. 16

This idea has been covered already at length. The phrase "the seed of Abraham" is a way of saying that Christ was born a Jewish man as opposed to becoming an angel. Disregard any hyper-Calvinist claptrap that tries to make this Abraham's *spiritual* seed. It is plainly referring to the Incarnation. God chose Abraham's family to be the one out of which the Redeemer would spring.

> *"Wherefore in all things it behoved him to be made like unto his brethren, that he might be a merciful and faithful high priest in things pertaining to God, to make reconciliation for the sins of the people. For in that he himself hath suffered being tempted, he is able to succour them that are tempted."* vv. 17-18

In verse 11, we saw that Christ was sanctified, or 'set apart' for His earthly service to God. We believe that God, through past ages, had many good priests that tried their best to serve Him faithfully, but we also have the testimony of Scripture against some that failed. In the Good Samaritan parable of Luke 10, the priest in verse

31 was so sanctified that he dared not defile himself to help the man that was half dead. God save us from such an attitude. The Old Testament priests may have served a function of reconciliation, but they were not characterized by compassion. But Jesus, our superior High Priest, not only reconciled us to God, but sympathizes with us on our own level, for He was willing to come where we were. He subjected Himself to our trials and tribulations so that He might 'bear with us' in our trouble. This is far beyond what was required by the mechanical functions of the priests of old time.

Eli's sons were utter failures as priests. They did things *while in the priestly office* that were heinous, and in public view. But an unnamed man of God, in pronouncing their judgment, gave this beautiful prophecy:

> *"And this shall be a sign unto thee, that shall come upon thy two sons, on Hophni and Phinehas; in one day they shall die both of them. And I will raise me up a faithful priest, that shall do according to that which is in mine heart and in my mind: and I will build him a sure house; and he shall walk before mine anointed for ever."* I Samuel 2:34-5.

Notice that He would do all that was in God's heart as well as His mind. God is the 'God of all comfort' (II Cor. 1:3). Christ was sanctified for this purpose in addition to reconciliation. We are sanctified for the 'ministry of reconciliation' (II Cor,

5:18), but we must not forget to follow Christ's example in this as well. F. B. Meyer said, "Suffering educates sympathy."[55] When we suffer trials, it is natural to ask ourselves or God "Why?" The answer might just be that being tried, we may be able, as representatives of Christ, to succor others. When extending sympathy, the past sufferings of the comforter are a benefit to the comforted.

---

[55] Meyer, F.B., *The Way Into the Holiest* (Zondervan, 1950), p. 36.

HEBREWS CHAPTER 3

"He turned and faced, not the blinding storm, but the trembling men, and said: 'O ye of little faith.' Unbelief! That was more terrible to Him than the storm; that called for more rebuke than the tempest."[56]

"Wherefore, holy brethren, partakers of the heavenly calling, consider the Apostle and High Priest of our profession, Christ Jesus;" Hebrews 3:1

"Wherefore," – Because of everything that has been written to this point (Chapters 1 & 2), consider *what is to follow.*

"holy brethren, partakers of the heavenly calling" – This is proof of the fact stated in the introduction that the addressees were saved people. Kenneth Wuest says, "The word 'holy' here does not have particular reference to a quality of life, but a position in salvation."[57] This will become important when we reach passages that are difficult to interpret and appear to suggest that a saved individual can become lost. Some commentators have solved these problem passages by saying the people referred to were not really saved to begin with. This is not the case, and the truth is more beautiful and more satisfying than such 'easy out' solutions.

---

[56] Haldeman, I.M. *The Tabernacle-Priesthood and Offerings* (Revell, New Jersey, 1925), p. 115.
[57] Wuest, *Hebrews*, p. 68.

These *'holy brethren'* are *'partakers of the heavenly calling.'* This phrase warrants some explanation because of how word meanings have changed. This shift in usage causes some to become dissatisfied with the term 'partakers.' 'Partners'[58] is used, as well as 'sharers,'[59] and such like. To be a 'partaker' is to 'take part.' 'Partners' is fine, but it doesn't tell the whole story. Nor does 'sharers.' The best way to think of 'partakers' is to think of what we mean when we used to say we 'partake' of a meal. One meal is served, and those at the table are partakers. The meal is consumed, each person taking a serving from each disparate dish. In this way, each individual diner has partaken of the whole meal. When you get Christ, you have access to everything He has to offer, if you are willing. Christ is not broken up in pieces, with each Christian gaining only a small part, like picking from a passing tray of hors d'oeuvres.

What of this 'heavenly calling?' There are attempts to explain it on its own terms, as these two words occur together only here, but the best description comes from the Bible's own use of the terms. 'Calling,' a noun (as in 'found one's calling'), is used in the Bible to denote God's purpose for His children in their life. Examples are I Corinthians 1:26, Ephesians 1:18 and 4:4, Philippians 3:14, II Thessalonians 1:11, I Timothy 1:9, and II Peter 1:10. Once it is used to describe one's occupation as well as God's will (I Corinthians 7:20-24). The

---

[58] Hobbs, *Hebrews*, p. 30.
[59] Barclay, *Hebrews*, p. 21.

point of the passage is to perform both at the same time.

A.C. Gaebelein said: "They are called "partakers of the heavenly calling" in contrast with their former "earthly calling" of Israel.[60] The 'calling' is 'heavenly' because of where it originated from, and because of where it will culminate. The best description available comes from the book of Second Timothy:

> *"Be not thou therefore ashamed of the testimony of our Lord, nor of me his prisoner: but be thou partaker of the afflictions of the gospel according to the power of God; Who hath saved us, and called us with an holy calling, not according to our works, but according to his own purpose and grace, which was given us in Christ Jesus before the world began, But is now made manifest by the appearing of our Saviour Jesus Christ, who hath abolished death, and hath brought life and immortality to light through the gospel:"* II Timothy 1:8-10

God's will is that every man, woman, and child come to a knowledge of the truth. His means are the testimony of those who know that truth. If you are saved, God had a purpose for your life in Christ before the world began. You will find no greater fulfillment in this life than finding and carrying out this eternal purpose.

------

[60] Gaebelein, *Annotated Bible*, p. 251. See also Wuest, *Hebrews,* p. 68.

> *"consider the Apostle and High Priest of our profession, Christ Jesus; Who was faithful to him that appointed him, as also Moses was faithful in all his house."* v. 1b-2

We have seen how Christ is superior to the patriarchs, superior to angels, superior to man as he was meant to be, superior to the Creation, and superior to the priesthood (albeit only briefly). The author of Hebrews now takes aim at one of the primary heroes of the Jewish people: Moses. This comparison was not without warrant, as the Jewish Bible (the Old Testament) put Moses alongside Christ in Deuteronomy 18:15:

> *"The LORD thy God will raise up unto thee a Prophet from the midst of thee, of thy brethren, like unto me; unto him ye shall hearken;"*

The appellation 'Apostle' means 'one sent forth.'[61] 'High Priest' refers to Christ's present office as Mediator between the believer and God. Further comparison will be made between Christ and the high priest of the Old Testament later; the purpose here is to show how Christ is superior to Moses, who had the same mission. Moses was faithful in what God called him to do (Numbers 7:12), yet imperfectly. Moses was sent forth, not only to redeem Israel out of Egypt, which he did, but also to usher them into the Promised Land (Exodus 3:8 with Numbers 20:12), an honor forfeited by Moses and given to Joshua. The high priesthood was accomplished through Aaron, not Moses. God had

---

[61] Newell, *Hebrews*, p. 80. See also Vine's.

a special typological purpose for both of these things. Most importantly, the administrative duties of the nation, or Moses' 'house,' were left to Moses, and he eventually delegated even this through the prodding of his father-in-law. God, however, considers Moses faithful, and this should be an encouragement for us. You will fail at times, but you may still be counted faithful.

Now consider Christ. Christ accomplished everything the Father gave Him to do, down to the last dotted 'i'. When He said, *"It is finished."* (John 19:30) It was! In the vernacular of this writer's high school basketball teammates, "He went *all the way*!" He left it all on the field. Nothing was undone.

> *"For this man was counted worthy of more glory than Moses, inasmuch as he who hath builded the house hath more honour than the house."* v. 3

God (Jesus) built the house and placed Moses over it, therefore He *has* to be superior. This may seem obvious, but it is a point of logic which must be borne out.

> *"For every house is builded by some man; but he that built all things is God. And Moses verily was faithful in all his house, as a servant, for a testimony of those things which were to be spoken after;"* vv. 4-5

Forgive us for working in reverse order here. *"a testimony of those things which were to be spoken after"* is the testimony of Moses against the religious leaders of Jesus' day. Christ brings up

Moses almost twenty times as recorded in the Gospels. Here is a perfect example:

> *"Do not think that I will accuse you to the Father: there is one that accuseth you, even Moses, in whom ye trust. For had ye believed Moses, ye would have believed me: for he wrote of me."* John 5:45-46.

In other words, the high regard in which the religious leaders held Moses made his testimony the perfect example to illustrate their unfaithfulness and unwillingness to accept His Messiahship.

Like the condescension of God to man in Christ, both Moses and Christ condescended to servanthood in their ministry. Any one of us can think of a pastor somewhere who was unwilling to follow Christ in this way. The trouble with some ministers is that they are unwilling to minister, taking in the accolades that come with being a polished preacher and prominent person, but not taking the time to get his hands dirty. This admonition is for every Christian. Finally, the first phrase is simply another equation of Christ with God.

> *"But Christ as a son over his own house; whose house are we, if we hold fast the confidence and the rejoicing of the hope firm unto the end."* v. 6

The final verse in this small section is one of the infamous sticky spots in this book. It is used by Arminians as well as 'moderate dispensationalists' to demonstrate that one can lose their salvation.

This can be dealt with rather easily, but as in any of the sticky spots we will encounter in this study, we should ask the question: "Does this verse state that *salvation* is lost?" Read it again. *"But Christ a son over his own house; saved are we, if we hold fast the confidence and rejoicing of the hope firm unto the end."* Not so. None of the 'questionable verses' mention salvation. This is a classic case of hopping on a hobby horse and riding away into the sunset, leaving the context in the dust. The immediate context is Christ versus Moses. Both have 'houses.' The children of Israel were Moses' house, we are Christ's. To make a one-to-one correspondence (as we believe the Holy Spirit is trying to do), we should be looking at what this text is saying Moses' house was, so we can apply it to ourselves as Christ's house.

We saw three things about Moses in verse 2. He was faithful, though imperfect in mission (apostle), priesthood, and administration. He was faithful, though everyone in the house was not. If a person was to be 'put out' of that economy (through leprosy or some other problem), He was still a Hebrew, but he lost out on the benefit of Moses' ministry in these three areas. (1) He missed out on his inheritance (Remember that only Joshua and Caleb made it into the Promised Land from the generation that left Egypt). (2) He missed out on the relationship to God afforded by the priesthood and the sacrificial system. (3) Thirdly, they ceased to live according to the administration of their leader, Moses. They lost inheritance, fellowship, and the opportunity to serve. This is exactly what we lose if we fail to *"hold fast the confidence and rejoicing of the hope firm unto the end."* We are a priesthood of believers, and we must not fail in our priestly duties.

> "When we withdraw from the exercise of our priestly New Testament worship, we are no longer fellowshipping with the other believers. But this does not mean we are not saved or that we had salvation and lost it."[62]

When we come across these tough places, we need to be clear on what is being said and what is not being said, and to stay in context. This kind of issue will arise several more times in Hebrews and will be treated in the same manner.

> *"Wherefore (as the Holy Ghost saith, To day if ye will hear his voice, Harden not your hearts, as in the provocation, in the day of temptation in the wilderness: When your fathers tempted me, proved me, and saw my works forty years. Wherefore I was grieved with that generation, and said, They do alway err in their heart; and they have not known my ways. So I sware in my wrath, They shall not enter into my rest.)"* vv. 7-8

Here we are amid the second of five warning or exhortation passages. If you will recall, the first was in 2:1-4, and bid us keep fresh in our minds the revelation of Christ as superior in His person. It was a reminder of our security in Him because of belief, pointing toward our *past* sanctification,

---

[62] Dillow, Joseph C., *The Reign of the Servant Kings* (Schoettle Publishing, 1992), p. 458.

which we called 'justification' in our chart on the three tenses of salvation. This warning deals with our *present* sanctification and service.

The author again refers to the Jewish Holy Book, this time quoting from Psalm 95. The express purpose is to warn Christians (for such were his readers) against something that pertained directly to them, using the Scriptures. There was direct application to them personally, to us, and to those future saints who will face the Tribulation and Second Coming. Don't listen to anyone who tells you there is no direct application to you.

> *"Moreover, brethren, I would not that ye should be ignorant, how that all our fathers were under the cloud, and all passed through the sea; And were all baptized unto Moses in the cloud and in the sea; And did all eat the same spiritual meat; And did all drink the same spiritual drink: for they drank of that spiritual Rock that followed them: and that Rock was Christ. But with many of them God was not well pleased: for they were overthrown in the wilderness. Now these things were our examples, to the intent we should not lust after evil things, as they also lusted. Neither be ye idolaters, as were some of them; as it is written, The people sat down to eat and drink, and rose up to play. Neither let us commit fornication, as some of them committed, and fell in one day three and twenty thousand. Neither let us tempt Christ, as some of them also tempted, and were destroyed of serpents. Neither murmur*

ye, as some of them also murmured, and were destroyed of the destroyer. Now all these things happened unto them for ensamples: and they are written for our admonition, upon whom the ends of the world are come." I Corinthians 10:1-11

This passage was written by Paul, the apostle to the Gentiles, to church-age Christians. It applies to us as surely as any other saved individual who reads the book of Hebrews.

This warning is against the 'hardening of the heart,' and against unbelief. This hardening of the heart is not hypertrophic cardiomyopathy (the hardening of the physical heart muscle), but a spiritual condition arising from the persistent refusal to heed the prodding of the Holy Spirit. The end result is that the hardened heart is "given over" by God. In other words, there comes a point of no return. There is a time limit. You can watch this process unfold in Exodus 7 as Pharaoh refuses God's message through Moses. He hardens his heart repeatedly until God finally hardens it. You can watch as the children of Israel murmur against God repeatedly, despite His very real and tangible presence among them, as well as His constant provision.

What is the message for us; the one that spans all of time (every dispensation)? Respond to God's pleading in your heart! Don't smother conviction. Seek to be sensitive to the Holy Spirit when He calls, for ignoring Him will cause His voice to become fainter; not because He isn't inside you, but because ignoring Him causes the heart to harden.

As stated above, the warning is for everyone, from the referents of Psalm 95, the hearers of Psalm 95, the readers of Hebrews, church-age Christians (you and me), and future believers including Jewish tribulation saints. The consequences of not heeding may be different, but the parallels, the types are concordant. They will not be broken.

So, to unravel this portion and to reveal its beautiful truths, we will treat it precisely as we did the first six verses of chapter 3. We will see <u>exactly</u> what is said, we will look at what it refers to <u>in context</u> and glean what the Holy Spirit intended us to glean.

"Wherefore I was grieved with that generation, and said, They do alway err in their heart; and they have not known my ways. So I sware in my wrath, They shall not enter into my rest.) Take heed, brethren, lest there be in any of you an evil heart of unbelief, in departing from the living God. But exhort one another daily, while it is called To day; lest any of you be hardened through the deceitfulness of sin. For we are made partakers of Christ, if we hold the beginning of our confidence stedfast unto the end; While it is said, To day if ye will hear his voice, harden not your hearts, as in the provocation. For some, when they had heard, did provoke: howbeit not all that came out of Egypt by Moses. But with whom was

he grieved forty years? was it not with them that had sinned, whose carcases fell in the wilderness?" vv. 9-17

The "Wherefore" takes from what is before (verses 3-6), and points to verse 12, but we must deal with the parenthesis that is here inserted. Knowing the meaning of the hardening of the heart, let's look at the culmination of Israel's hard-heartedness, the rebellion at Kadesh Barnea in Numbers 13 and 14. All of Israel's 'trying' of God came to a head here. God allowed Moses to send twelve spies into Canaan to search it out. When they returned, ten of the spies discouraged the people with a negative report. Two of the spies-Joshua and Caleb-gave a good report, but they were not heeded. This caused the people to refuse entry into Canaan. Not only that, but they sought to return to Egypt (14:4). Because of this, God struck the ten bad spies with a plague, and the people wandered in the wilderness for forty years; one year for every day they were in the land. They never entered the "rest" spoken of in verse 8 of our text. This is sad enough, yet if it weren't for the intercession of Moses (14:14-19), they would have been dead (14:12). *Please note God would take their physical life before He would let them return to Egypt.*

According to some, this passage has absolutely nothing to do with church-age believers, and further, that is different from the "rest" of the next chapter and has nothing to do with any other "rest" in Scripture.[63] This is not true at all. Every mention of "rest" in the Bible is intimately related and connected in a beautiful, God-glorifying way. He is not the author of confusion (I Corinthians 14:33).

Let's look at some of the components of this story and see how it relates to us directly.

Children of Israel	Children of God
Redeemed from Egypt	Delivered from the world
By the Pascal Lamb	By Christ, the Lamb of God
Passed through Jordan	Baptized 'into Christ'
Called to Canaan and "rest"	Called to sanctification and victory
Faced a voluntary choice to enter	Faced with a voluntary choice to enter

As you can see from the table above, our deliverance and Christian journey directly parallels Israel's. So why would the failure to live up to their calling not line up as well? And why would the author of Hebrews give an example from God's word that wasn't appropriate to the situation? The answer is that he wouldn't. To do so would be to mishandle the word of truth.

---

[63] Ruckman, *Hebrews*, p. 87.

Children of Israel	Children of God
Failure to enter Canaan	Failure to enter 'abundant life'
Hardening of heart	Hardening of heart
Wilderness wandering	Spiritual wandering
Loss of inheritance	Loss of inheritance

There are things that change with the advent of new dispensations, but the primary truths remain the same. Here are those truths across the ages:

Children of Israel	Readers of Hebrews	Children of God	Tribulation Saints
Death in the wilderness	Death in the siege of Jerusalem A.D. 70	Chastening of God, including possible death	Death by persecution, etc.
Loss of spiritual and physical inheritance	Loss of spiritual and Millennial inheritance	Loss of spiritual and Millennial inheritance	Loss of spiritual and Millennial inheritance
Salvation of the soul	Salvation of the soul	Salvation of the soul	Salvation of the soul

The judgments varied. The object warned against did not. Some were told to enter the Promised Land (Numbers), some were told to stay away (Hebrews). But there is a bottom line here. It is that disobedience to God brings consequences. Among these, at least for the child of God, is not condemnation in Hell. Remember, God would not let them go back to Egypt. An Israelite in bondage in Egypt was a picture of someone lost and enslaved to sin. The consequences of those that believe were an entrance into what God calls "rest." Those who believed God and entered were Joshua and Caleb. What is the ratio of Christians who drift through life, stifling the Holy Spirit, and never doing anything meaningful for God, to those who follow Him wholeheartedly? The latter will be those who will fully 'partake of Christ' (experience all He has to offer).

> *"And to whom sware he that they should not enter into his rest, but to them that believed not? So we see that they could not enter in because of unbelief."* vv. 18-19

It is important to note that belief, and not works of any kind, was the condition of obedience. Belief was what was employed when the Holy Spirit convicted the unsaved heart, that caused the lost soul to make the choice between God and everything else in the universe; to place his faith in Christ for his eternal destiny. Likewise, it is belief that will spur the believer on to good works, the purpose for which he or she was saved. Our text is urging the readers to believe; to rest in what Christ has done regarding their salvation, and not go back to a religion of dead works. It must be some form of unbelief that is keeping Christians from serving God the way He wants them to.

Now let's talk about what the "rest" actually is. Rest is not a cessation from work. The children of Israel still had to conquer the cities of Canaan when they got across the river. God created, then *"rested on the seventh day"* (Genesis 2:2-3). Did God stop working? When persecuted by the Pharisees for doing a miracle on the sabbath, Jesus responded like this: *"But Jesus answered them, My Father worketh hitherto, and I work."* John 5:17. Was it God's purpose that man should do nothing at all while on the sabbath? No! So, what's the deal? It was a sign (Exodus 31:13). It looked forward to something. It is all wrapped up in Christ's complete work of redemption. The sabbath at the end of the creation week was a foreshadowing of the week of Christ's redemptive work. He followed a pattern that occurred during Creation and Passover that took a week to complete. After the Resurrection, He told Mary He must ascend to heaven. This was to perform His High Priestly work. At the end of Creation, God's work was completed, and He rested (not because He was tired...). Does this mean God was done working? Passover was a week-long event followed by a Sabbath of rest. There are many more types to support this. After the Flood, the ark 'rested.' When the Temple was completed, the ark of the testimony 'rested.' The rest the believer enters in this life is not a rest from 'good works,' but a rest from reliance on good works to earn what God has already promised to give. It is an insult to God in this, or any dispensation to try to offer Him our filthy works in exchange for His salvation.

> "As to the 'works' from which we rest, the similarity with God's works is simply this: as God set (H)imself a task to perform during the six days of creation and, when (H)e had finished it, rested in the contemplation of (H)is work and its glorious perfection, so we have a task set for us, a vocation assigned us by God as (H)is people, and when we complete it we are made partakers of (H)is rest with all that means of heavenly satisfaction and joy ... God's rest is not idleness, nor shall ours be when we enter (H)is rest."[64]

The "rest" that the children of Israel missed out on included fighting. God wanted His chosen land rid of all the evil, idolatrous, deviant, murderous people that festered within it. To refuse to enter meant to refuse to fight. Our "rest" is similar in this way: We are in a battle. The easy way out (at least on the surface) would be to lay back and let others do the work of God. This is exactly how you refuse to enter rest. You either don't believe God will do anything about it, or you don't believe it makes a difference. God swore against Israel in His wrath. How do you think you're doing? Even if God were to spare you in this life, heed I Corinthians 3:9-15:

> *"For we are labourers together with God: ye are God's husbandry, ye are God's building. According to the grace of God which*

---

[64] Lenski, Richard C. H., *The Interpretation of the Epistle to the Hebrews and the Epistle of James* (Augsburg Publishing House, 1963), p. 138.

is given unto me, as a wise masterbuilder, I have laid the foundation, and another buildeth thereon. But let every man take heed how he buildeth thereupon. For other foundation can no man lay than that is laid, which is Jesus Christ. Now if any man build upon this foundation gold, silver, precious stones, wood, hay, stubble; Every man's work shall be made manifest: for the day shall declare it, because it shall be revealed by fire; and the fire shall try every man's work of what sort it is. If any man's work abide which he hath built thereupon, he shall receive a reward. If any man's work shall be burned, he shall suffer loss: but he himself shall be saved; yet so as by fire."

Lastly, when the children of Israel went into the land, what kind of 'work' did they actually do? Think about Jericho. They marched around seven times (there's that seven again!). The walls fell and they went and claimed the spoils. Think of Ai. The defeat caused by Achan's sin cost them 36 men. We know that every life is precious, but from a military standpoint, 36 is nothing compared to the hundreds of thousands they were taking out. They got depressed about it because they hadn't been losing any! What's the point for us? It was not so much the Israelites that fought, but God fought *for* them. The same is true of our abundant Christian life. Christ does the work *through* us, and then shares the reward with us.

HEBREWS CHAPTER 4

"John Henry told his captain,
'A man ain't nothing but a man,
But before I'll let that steam drill beat me down
I'll die with a hammer in my hand, Lord, Lord,
I'll die with a hammer in my hand.'"
American Folk Song

"Let us therefore fear, lest, a promise being left us of entering into his rest, any of you should seem to come short of it."
Hebrews 4:1

The 'rest' referred to here is still the rest that comes with the victorious Christian life—the 'life more abundantly' of John 10:10. There will be another rest introduced in verse 9. Though different, the two 'rests' are intertwined inexorably. To eliminate confusion between 'rests' we provide this illustration, related to the three 'tenses' of salvation

[See the table on the next page]

Rest of Salvation	Rest of Sanctification	Rest of Glorification
Past	Present	Future
Rest from work to earn escape from Hell and reconciliation with God	Rest resulting from living the Christian life in the power of the Spirit/ Christ living *through* you	Rest during the Millennium, inheritance of rewards for service during this life
Called Salvation (Rom. 10:13)	Called Salvation (Rom. 5:13, II Thess. 2:13)	Called Salvation (Romans 13:11, I Thess. 5:9)

It should be clear that what is fallen short of is not escape from Hell and reconciliation with God, or what is commonly called 'salvation.' It is entry into the abundant Christian life. There are those who still labor to secure their own salvation. This is humans trying to do something Christ already did. Do we think God lied? Do we think we can do it better?

> *"Are ye so foolish? having begun in the Spirit, are ye now made perfect by the flesh?"* Galatians 3:3

The 'rest' in the first half of this chapter is similar. Although saved, and seemingly secure in their salvation, there are those who still labor to gain acceptance with God. They are either working to avoid some kind of punishment or to atone for some past wrong. Both are sinful. Christ paid for all sins, past and present. You don't have to 'win' God's acceptance; you are already 'accepted in the beloved' through Christ's finished work (Ephesians 1:6)!

The present tense 'rest' of this verse is a result of operating under the power of the Holy Spirit, and Christ accomplishing His work through us who believe.

> *"For unto us was the gospel preached, as well as unto them: but the word preached did not profit them, not being mixed with faith in them that heard it." v. 2*

The problem now, just as then, is unbelief. Do we really believe Christ has secured our salvation for us? If so, we can then live in confidence, not looking at God as though He is waiting for us to mess up so He can jerk back His salvation.

Even so, present tense salvation is a matter of belief. Let's get real practical for a minute. Sometimes our kids are hard to love. They simply aren't angels 100% of the time, but they are ours. They will not lose their position. What about other people's kids? What about 'bus kids?' Can we love them as we ought, or are we tempted to let frustration and even contempt build up? Are we ready to let them go, or refuse them the Gospel? The problem with trying to love any kid (or an adult for that matter) who is unruly is that *we* are trying to love them. We need to try to let Jesus Christ love them *through* us. The hits we take as a result are to be reckoned *His* hits. The sacrifice is made for Him. It should flow from an appreciation of the work He has already done. Do you see how it is a matter of belief?

> *"I am crucified with Christ: nevertheless I live; yet not I, but Christ liveth in me: and the life which I now live in the flesh I live by the faith of the Son of God, who loved me, and gave himself for me."* Galatians 2:20

> *"For we which have believed do enter into rest, as he said, As I have sworn in my wrath, if they shall enter into my rest: although the works were finished from the foundation of the world. For he spake in a certain place of the seventh day on this wise, And God did rest the seventh day from all his works. And in this place again, If they shall enter into my rest. Seeing therefore it remaineth that some must enter therein, and they to whom it was first preached entered not in because of unbelief:"* vv. 3-6

These verses express the fact that God preordained the rest that the children of Israel should have entered, as well as the rest we should enter as Christians, the proof being the rest He took after Creation. The fact that God is all-powerful (omnipotent) means He didn't need seven days to create the universe. He could have done it instantly (see Genesis 1:16). He took six days on purpose, and He rested on the seventh day for a purpose. Christ's redemptive work took seven days on purpose. The wilderness crossing should have taken seven days. God's plan since before the Creation has been for His people to operate on the basis of the cross. This is something they were chosen for but neglected. Many things were predestined for the Hebrew people, but they missed out for unbelief.

> "The promise God made to Israel refers to the nation *as a people* – not to individuals, and not necessarily to *all Israel*. When Israel sees the Lord in His second coming, they will fall down and worship Him. There will be a definite fulfillment of the promises God made to Abraham, and a nation will be born in a day…The promise concerning Canaan did not necessarily refer to the people led out of Egypt by Moses – to *all* of them or to *any* of that particular generation. If God's promise had been an absolute, unconditional promise to that specific generation, then it would have been a divine necessity that the promise be fulfilled. Otherwise, God would have broken a promise – and that is impossible, for God cannot lie."[65]

This is a direct parallel to the way His people are 'predestined' today. It is God's will that His people live in the power of the cross by belief. Not all do, but like the children of Israel, there will be Joshuas and Calebs, and the failure or success of the parents does not guarantee the failure or

---

[65] Greene, *Hebrews,* p. 126.

success of the children. Romans 11 is about God's chosen people:

> *"Lord, they have killed thy prophets, and digged down thine altars; and I am left alone, and they seek my life. But what saith the answer of God unto him? I have reserved to myself seven thousand men, who have not bowed the knee to the image of Baal. Even so then at this present time also there is a remnant according to the election of grace."* Romans 11:3-5

Thank God if you belong to a good church, because 'Christendom' as a whole is a dismal failure. The largest 'Protestant' denomination in America is saddled with egalitarianism, LGBTQ issues, money and sex scandals, abuse, and general apostasy. Earnest Christians will always be in the minority.

Note that the fact that all did not enter Canaan did not negate Moses' faithfulness, nor did Israel's incomplete subjugation of Canaan negate Joshua's. Romans 11 goes on to say Israel's rejection of their Messiah did not negate God's faithfulness, and our failure to serve Him as we ought does not negate Christ's. All these things will be reconciled someday.

> *"Again, he limiteth a certain day, saying in David, To day, after so long a time; as it is said, To day if ye will hear his voice, harden not your hearts."* v. 7

The offer of rest for the children of Israel had a time limit on it. In the same way, our opportunity for Christian service has a time limit. Did you know the rapture of the church could happen at any moment? This is the so-called doctrine of 'Immanency.'

"I must work the works of him that sent me, while it is day: the night cometh, when no man can work." John 9:4

"But ye, brethren, are not in darkness, that that day should overtake you as a thief. Ye are all the children of light, and the children of the day: we are not of the night, nor of darkness. Therefore let us not sleep, as do others; but let us watch and be sober." I Thessalonians 5:4-6

Let us not forget that the readers of Hebrews had a time limit of their own. Had they chosen to return to Judaism at Jerusalem, they would have faced judgment from emperor Titus in A.D. 70.

"For if Jesus had given them rest, then would he not afterward have spoken of another day." v. 8

"Jesus" in this verse is the Greek transliteration of the Hebrew name 'Joshua.' The names mean "Jehovah is salvation." This solidifies the parallels we are observing. The "he" is David, the Psalmist, as we are still dealing with the passage from Psalm 95.

"There remaineth therefore a rest to the people of God." v. 9

"...there is still something more to be expected and experienced in the way of rest."[66]

There is always going to be 'something more' to the wonders of Christ. We who are saved found rest at conversion. After that, we can find rest in Christ for Christian living. We have the future promise of the dispensational sabbath, the Millennial reign of Christ, followed by the ultimate rest, eternal life in the new heavens and new earth, where the wonders will never cease. The deeper you go, the longer you serve, the more you learn, and the more you rest, "the sweeter He grows!"

> *"For he that is entered into his rest, he also hath ceased from his own works, as God did from his. Let us labour therefore to enter into that rest, lest any man fall after the same example of unbelief."* vv. 10-11

With this, our author ties his exposition of Psalm 95 up with a beautiful bow, exhorting his readers to heed the 'ensample' (I Corinthians 10:11) and enter spiritual rest. *"Let us labor..."* proves once and for all that this rest cannot be the rest of conversion (Romans 11:6, Ephesians 2:8,9).

> *"For the word of God is quick, and powerful, and sharper than any twoedged sword, piercing even to the dividing asunder of soul and spirit, and of the joints and marrow, and is a discerner of the thoughts*

---

[66] Griffith Thomas, *Go On*, p. 49.

and intents of the heart. Neither is there any creature that is not manifest in his sight: but all things are naked and opened unto the eyes of him with whom we have to do." vv. 12-13

"Quick" here means living, as in *"the quick and the dead"* (I Peter 4:5).

This passage is very popular amongst King James Bible defenders, and for good reason. It extolls the nature of the Holy Bible. It is quoted so very often in isolation that it is unintentionally lifted from its context. The context is judgment:

> "And we need to remember that God's Word is ever the standard of judgment, and not our knowledge of it"[67]

This is appropriate because our Christian lives are going to be judged at the Judgment Seat of Christ, just prior to entering the Millennium. It will determine our reward going into the kingdom. It MUST refer to this judgment, because the author of Hebrews is writing to Christians, and not lost people. Failing to identify this causes great confusion.

> "We cannot but notice how intimately the written Word and the Eternal Word are linked together."[68]

Think back to the beginning of our study. *"God, who at sundry times and in divers manners*

---

[67] Ironside, *Hebrews and Titus*, p. 60.
[68] Ibid.

spake in time past unto the fathers by the prophets, Hath in these last days spoken unto us by his Son" Hebrews 1:1-2. God has spoken by His Son, the Word made flesh (John 1), and we will be judged *by* the Word, *from* the Word, according to what we did *with* the Word.

> *"Seeing then that we have a great high priest, that is passed into the heavens, Jesus the Son of God, let us hold fast our profession."* v. 14

To unfold the truths of the magnificent book of Hebrews, we have (1) kept in mind the theme, (2) made comparisons between the Old Testament types and their modern-day applications, and (3) moved slowly, giving attention to exactly what is written. This was the author's (and the Holy Spirit's) intention and is the key to proper interpretation. This mode continues as we take our second, and closer, look at our Great High Priest, the Lord Jesus Christ.

Remember that the first mention of Christ's High Priesthood in the book of Hebrews was at 2:17:

> *"Wherefore in all things it behoved him to be made like unto his brethren, that he might be a merciful and faithful high priest in things pertaining to God, to make reconciliation for the sins of the people."*

"The reason for returning to the idea of the high priestly duties now is because of what has just been said in verses 4:12, 13. Man is

completely open and exposed before God,
to whom we must give an account."[69]

It could be argued that 2:17 be tied to the sin offering, for it reconciled them to God, whereas 4:14-16 speaks of the other offerings of Leviticus, for they speak of consecration and praise.

There are many wonderful and astounding things to learn about the Old Testament priesthood, and we will see some of that in time, but the purpose of this particular passage is to give yet another superiority of Christ over the Aaronic priesthood. With that in mind, we should have a general idea as to what the high priest did, and what that means for us.

The priests of the Old Testament ministered to God on behalf of the people of Israel (Exodus 28:1). God consecrated the sons of Aaron as priests, and Aaron himself as high priest. All were anointed and wore special garments (Exodus 28:3). These priests were mediators in the sense that they facilitated proper worship for the people, and created a condition where God could dwell among His people (Exodus 25:8). Israel's proper worship was a condition for God's blessing upon them, as was their denial of the sins of the wicked people around them (Exodus 19:5). God wanted their heart, and He provided a way to Himself through the priesthood.

But why this separation? Why was there a gap between God and man? Why did man have to

---

[69] Garrett and Voitenko, p. 128.

jump through all these hoops to get to God? It is because of sin. God is holy and there can be no sin in his presence. There was a time when God walked with man in the cool of the day. God blessed man and gave him everything he needed. One day God went to the place where He and man met together, and the man wasn't there. Sin had entered and caused separation. This took place in Genesis 3.

So, it is important to know that sacrifice is the condition whereby sin is dealt with so that God and man may commune. Please note that salvation is not the issue at hand. The high priest of the Old Testament didn't save anyone. The sacrifices of the law didn't save anyone. They were for God's blessing and presence in the lives of His people, and to typify the work which the great High Priest would one day accomplish.

> ". . .the Passover was the sacrifice by which an enslaved and doomed people obtained redemption, whereas, in common with the other sacrifices of the law, the sin offering was for those who had thus been redeemed."[70]

Jesus Christ took the role of sacrifice as regards our salvation. Now, in His current office of the High Priest of our profession, He is our Daysman. He has fulfilled all of the requirements for us to commune with God.

So, why the distinction of "High Priest?" There are two reasons that lie right on the surface,

---

[70] Anderson, *Types*, p. 50.

and they are the most important for our purposes now.

(1) The high priest of the Old Testament had a particular rite to accomplish on the Day of Atonement, called Yom Kippur today. You can read about this in Leviticus 16, and it will be dealt with more thoroughly when we reach chapter 9 of Hebrews. This was on behalf of the people, and typified something only Christ could accomplish in reality.

(2) The high priest had a unique office separate from the rest of the priests in this sense: He equipped, anointed, and applied blood to the other priests, preparing them for their service to God. This is critical to understanding God's reasons for setting things up this way. We who are saved are priests.

> *"Ye also, as lively stones, are built up a spiritual house, an holy priesthood, to offer up spiritual sacrifices, acceptable to God by Jesus Christ."* I Peter 2:5

And again,

> *"But ye are a chosen generation, a royal priesthood, an holy nation, a peculiar people; that ye should shew forth the praises of him who hath called you out of darkness into his marvellous light:"* verse 9 of that same chapter.

We no longer need men as mediators between us and God!

"For there is one God, and one mediator between God and men, the man Christ Jesus;" I Timothy 2:5

It is therefore to be rejected any religious system that has an earthly priesthood that stands between God and men! There are duties that fall to God's people, echoed by the work of the priesthood, and the rest is accomplished by Christ. Everyone else is out of a job.

"For we have not an high priest which cannot be touched with the feeling of our infirmities; but was in all points tempted like as we are, yet without sin. Let us therefore come boldly unto the throne of grace, that we may obtain mercy, and find grace to help in time of need." vv. 15-16

So, just what is it that makes Christ superior as a High Priest? The first is the location of the execution of His High priestly duty. Verse 14 says, *"that is passed into the heavens."* God met with the Old Testament high priest in a tent first, then a room of a building. This is called the 'most holy place.' These were only rudimentary pictures, or stand-ins for the throne room of God. On the Day of Atonement, the priest would offer a sacrifice on behalf of God's people and carry it into the most holy place and deposit it upon the mercy seat. This act 'atoned for' or covered the sins so that God could meet with them. The Day of Atonement pictured Christ entering into Heaven with His blood having just been shed and brought to God in order to purge the sins of His people. The Old Testament priest could only picture what Christ actually did.

Secondly, verse 14 seemingly goes out of the way to call Jesus Christ the *"Son of God."* Why go through the trouble? Jesus not only entered because of what He did, but because of Who He was. Think of Esther in Chapter 5 of the Book of Esther. Though she feared greatly, she purposed to enter and approach the throne, and favor was granted to her on the basis of who she was. If you had a relative in prison in Saudi Arabia, who better to appeal to the Crown Prince on behalf of this relative than the son of the Crown Prince? You seek to enter into God's presence with the knowledge of how holy He Is, and how sinful you are. Who better to represent you to God than His own Son, Jesus Christ?

Lastly for this section, Christ, because He became a man, can understand our infirmities, or weaknesses. This the priest of old could also do, but with one blessed difference. Christ was without sin. Before the priests could minister, they had to offer sin offerings for themselves. Remember, this did not picture salvation, but holiness. Christ did not need a sin offering, for He had no sin! This qualifies Him to enter on our behalf.

The text says He *"was in all points tempted like as we are,"*. What does this mean? The text is speaking of human infirmities. Purge from your mind any thought that Jesus, for one millisecond, gave any consideration to any sin. We have a corrupt idea of temptation in that we think temptation is brooding over sin and deciding whether we want to engage in it or not. The Bible says "The thought of foolishness *is* sin" in Proverbs 24:9. Christ was God in the flesh. He could not and would not have sinned, but He subjected Himself to human frailty in the sense that He experienced every feeling of weakness. He felt hunger and thirst, though He never could have died from starvation or dehydration. He felt compassion and anger, though He was always in full control of His faculties. He rested and slept, though He was completely omnipotent, and He felt the agony of death, though He never would have died had He not dismissed His spirit.

We are frail in that our weariness, hunger, thirst, or pain can cause us to act in ways we ordinarily wouldn't. We can get irritable and lash out. Christ went through all these things and passed through unscathed. It was not necessary that He confront every sin, but that He come face to face with everything that causes men (outside of their own sin nature) to sin and that He conquer. C. S. Lewis had this to say regarding temptation:

> "No man knows how bad he is till he has tried very hard to be good. A silly idea is current that good people do not know what temptation means. This is an obvious lie. Only those who try to resist temptation know how strong it is... A man who gives in to temptation after five minutes simply does not know what it would have been like an hour later. That is why bad people, in one sense,

know very little about badness. They have
lived a sheltered life by always giving in."[71]

In this way Jesus knows more about
temptation than anyone else does; just don't make
the mistake of thinking that He really wanted to sin
and just didn't. He wasn't strong because He
resisted sin; His trials proved Him to be 'without
sin' in the eyes of all observers.

> "Sin was not a temptation to Him because
> there was nothing in Him to respond to it, but
> it undoubtedly caused suffering, which was
> all the more intense because He was
> sinless"[72]

It wasn't necessary that He go through
things to accomplish our redemption, but rather
that He bears with us now. Remember, this passage
is showing Christ as superior in His function as our
High Priest by comparing Him with the Old
Testament high priest.

You might be thinking, "If we have a High
Priest now, what exactly is different from the old
days?" Of course, we don't offer *physical* sacrifices.
I Peter 2:5 quoted above, refers to 'spiritual
sacrifices.' As we will see in Chapter 13 of Hebrews,
we offer God the sacrifice of praise. Intercessory
prayer is a sacrifice. We also have another sacrifice
to make, described in Romans 12:1:

---

[71]   Lewis, C.S., *Mere Christianity* (Macmillan
Publishing, 1952), p. 109-110.
[72] Griffith Thomas, *Go On*, p. 55.

> *"I beseech you therefore, brethren, by the mercies of God, that ye present your bodies a living sacrifice, holy, acceptable unto God, which is your reasonable service."*

These things have their parallels in the burning of incense and the burnt offerings of consecration respectively. The difference in our priesthood is that it is *spiritual.* Christ differed from the Old Testament high priest in that, as we have seen, (1) He was sinless, so no sin offering was needed for Him. Also, as we will see later, (2) He entered the *heavenly* most holy place *only once,* for His sacrifice was eternal instead of annual. And lastly, He did so to give us access to God, but now, because of this (3) we have free access to God based upon His work. This is the foundation that the book of Hebrews rests upon! The Old Testament priesthood could only offer *limited* access to God and win His blessings. Our High Priest made it so that we can enter the very throne room of God on the merits of His Son. This is why, in Matthew 27:51 the veil of the Temple that blocked the way to the most holy place was torn in two. The throne room is open. God's people may freely enter! This is a superb argument as to why the readers of Hebrews out to "hold fast their profession!"

There is such a contrast here. At Sinai, the people could not climb the mountain, and were even forbidden from touching it (Exodus 19:12-13)! Even the priests were forbidden from touching the implements of the tabernacle outside of their consecrated service (Numbers 4:15), à la Uzzah (II

Samuel 6). Even the high priest, if he entered the most holy place unworthily, or at the wrong time, he was dead (Leviticus 16:2).

O, let us not let the gentle graciousness of Christ cause us to lose our holy reverence for Godly service like it did for the Israelites.

Do not mistake the "boldness" of verse 16 with arrogance. Remember *"God resisteth the proud, but giveth grace unto the humble."* James 4:6b, and *"For all those things hath mine hand made, and all those things have been, saith the LORD: but to this man will I look, even to him that is poor and of a contrite spirit, and trembleth at my word."* Isaiah 66:2 We have both the privilege and the right to approach the throne of God because of Christ. This does not negate reverence. Remember Esther.

Jesus Christ entered the throne room of God and placed His blood there. It is on this basis that we have both received mercy and do request it now. It is on this basis that we receive grace when needed.

> "If you do commit sin, you must not be so much cast down, as if the door of mercy were clapped against you; no, there is an agent above to keep it open for every one that repents and believes."[73]

---

[73] Charnock, Stephen, *The Works of Stephen Charnock, Volume Five* (Banner of Truth Trust, 2021), p. 91.

"On the cross our Lord presented the sacrifice for sins. In Heaven now, He offers our gifts of worship and praise."[74]

"The law was given that every mouth may be (stopped), for we are guilty. The High Priest was given that every mouth may be open, for Jesus receive(s) sinners."[75]

Concerning the "grace to help in time of need," we will let Brother Paul testify:

"And lest I should be exalted above measure through the abundance of the revelations, there was given to me a thorn in the flesh, the messenger of Satan to buffet me, lest I should be exalted above measure. For this thing I besought the Lord thrice, that it might depart from me. And he said unto me, My grace is sufficient for thee: for my strength is made perfect in weakness. Most gladly therefore will I rather glory in my infirmities, that the power of Christ may rest upon me." II Corinthians 12:7-9

---

[74] Ironside, *Hebrews and Titus* (Loizeaux Bros., 1963), p. 69.

[75] Saphir, Adolph, *The Epistle to the Hebrews: An Exposition, Vol. 1* (Loizeaux Bros., 1946), p. 207.

HEBREWS CHAPTER 5

"Gentleman, this is a football" – Vince Lombardi[76]

"For every high priest taken from among men is ordained for men in things pertaining to God, that he may offer both gifts and sacrifices for sins: Who can have compassion on the ignorant, and on them that are out of the way; for that he himself also is compassed with infirmity. And by reason hereof he ought, as for the people, so also for himself, to offer for sins. And no man taketh this honour unto himself, but he that is called of God, as was Aaron." Hebrews 5:1-4

The opening verses of Hebrews 5 take off from the last three verses of Hebrews 4. Our author will continue to both compare and contrast the high priesthood of Christ with that of the other high priests, including Aaron, his descendants, and even Melchisedec. These verses are about Aaron and his line specifically. The Authorized Version is precise in its language, not lumping Christ in with these other priests because of verse 3. Christ is a High Priest, but unlike all the others, He does not have to offer the sin offering like the rest because He is completely apart from sin. Why mention this? Because there are translations which are not so scrupulous in this regard. Notice how the wording

---

[76] Mr. Lombardi said this to his Green Bay Packers in 1961, illustrating the need to return to the fundamentals.

is very similar, but does not place this critical separation between Christ and the others:

> "Every high priest is selected from among the people and is appointed to represent the people in matters related to God, to offer gifts and sacrifices for sins." Hebrews 5:1 NIV

Jesus Christ was not "selected from among the people" and did not have to offer the same sin offering.

Notice that the 'calling' of Aaron was an 'honour.' Aaron had a vocational election.

> *"So also Christ glorified not himself to be made an high priest; but he that said unto him, Thou art my Son, to day have I begotten thee. As he saith also in another place, Thou art a priest for ever after the order of Melchisedec."* vv. 5,6

Here is where Christ's part of the comparison comes in. Just like Aaron was selected for service on behalf of men by God, Christ was selected for service on behalf of mankind for God. These verses are from Psalm 2:7, and Psalm 110:4 respectively. Notice Christ "glorified not himself." The Holy Spirit glorifies Christ in John 16, and Christ glorifies the Father in John 17. It appears that humility is a trait of the God to Whom belongeth all praise!

> "The statement underscores not the grandeur of the office, but the humility required of the high priest, who receives his

office only through the appointment of God."[77]

"Who in the days of his flesh, when he had offered up prayers and supplications with strong crying and tears unto him that was able to save him from death, and was heard in that he feared; Though he were a Son, yet learned he obedience by the things which he suffered; And being made perfect, he became the author of eternal salvation unto all them that obey him;" vv. 7-9

The comparison of Christ in His High Priesthood with the Aaronic is critical to understanding what our author is trying to say here. Let's ask a few questions about this passage: Did Jesus need to be saved from death? Was He afraid of it? Can Jesus learn? Did He have to learn to obey? Was He not perfect until then?

Jesus is God. He did not need to be saved from death. He would not and could not have died until He gave up His Ghost. Rather, this is a reference to the Resurrection.

"Who by him do believe in God, that raised him up from the dead, and gave him glory; that your faith and hope might be in God." I Peter 1:21

Ironside says it plainly:

---

[77] Lane, William L. *Hebrews-A Call to Commitment* (Hendrickson, 1985), p. 79.

"For, be it observed, He was not saved *from* dying nor did He ever pray to be saved from death, nor did He fear death."[78]

Was He afraid of it? The passage says *He feared*. This is not the fear of someone afraid of dying. The 'fear' mentioned here is the reverence due to anyone who approaches God. Let us compare two ways the Bible uses the term 'fear.'

Fear 1

"Wherefore should I fear in the days of evil, when the iniquity of my heels shall compass me about?" Psalm 49:5

"In God I will praise his word, in God I have put my trust; I will not fear what flesh can do unto me." Psalm 56:4

Fear 2

"The fear of the LORD is clean, enduring for ever:" Psalm 19:9a.

"In the fear of the LORD is strong confidence: and his children shall have a place of refuge." Proverbs 14:26

"Surely his salvation is nigh them that fear him; that glory may dwell in our land." Psalm 85:9

Which of these two fears do you think Christ was displaying? Read the verses of your Bible where 'fear' is mentioned,

---

[78] Ironside, *Hebrews and Titus*, p. 70.

"Then shalt thou understand the fear of the LORD, and find the knowledge of God." Proverbs 2:5

One of God's primary attributes is His omniscience, meaning He knows all. Christ is also God and was still coequal even as a man. He did not lay aside His omniscience to become a man. Colossians 2:9 says, *"For in him dwelleth all the fulness of the Godhead bodily."* This makes it impossible that there be anything Jesus Christ did not know. Scholars through the centuries have struggled with this concept, however, and here is a sample of some things they have said:

Speaking of Christ's receiving the Holy Spirit at His baptism, Alfred Plummer wrote:

"But the new gift of the Spirit may have illuminated even Him, and made Him more fully aware of His relations to God and to man"[79]

Does this sound reasonable? Lorraine Boettner said:

"From the mouth of His mother He first learned the sacred things of God, and at her knee He often knelt to pray."[80]

---

[79] Plummer, Alfred, *An Exegetical Commentary on the Gospel According to St. Matthew* (Robert Scott, 1909), p. 34.

[80] Boettner, Lorraine, *Studies in Theology* (The Presbyterian and Reformed Publishing Company, 1947), p. 183.

This is a Protestant repeating Catholic tradition. Even the great William Evans drops the ball:

> "It seems clear, however, from the Scriptures, that we are to attribute Jesus' growth and advancement to the training He received in a godly home; to the instruction given at the synagogue and the temple; from His own personal study of the Scriptures, and from His fellowship and communion with His Father."[81]

Herschel Hobbs said that Jesus "struggled" to learn and did so continuously.[82] This begs the question: when did He reach perfection in knowledge? Did He ever? "Continuously" means He never stopped learning! The problem is that these men seem to not approach the Scripture with the fear and reverence described above. We, as men, are so bold and arrogant when it comes to these things. We career through Scripture like a young child in a museum, oblivious to the significance of most of what surrounds us, and touching things we ought not.

To assist you in gaining some reverence (which we all need), ask yourself these questions:

"Was Jesus God as a child?"

If not, "Who was He?"

---

[81] Evans, William, *The Great Doctrines of the Bible* (Moody Press, 1974), p. 55.

[82] Hobbs, Herschel, *Hebrews-Challenges to Bold Leadership* (Scripture Truth Book Co., 1971), p. 52.

If not, "When did He regain His Godhood?" Some have said at His baptism...Some have said after the Resurrection...

Omniscience means all-knowing. "How long did it take for Him to 'learn' infinite knowledge?"

"Was Mary or were the apostate Jews at the synagogue and Temple up to the task of teaching Him?"

"Did He suddenly realize, during His personal study of the Scriptures, 'O yeah, I remember telling Moses to write that!'?"

You see, the difference between Jesus Christ and us from a developmental and cognitive standpoint it that we were a brand-new mind being placed in an imperfect brain. He was a pre-existent, Infinite mind being installed in a perfect brain. We simply cannot take our sinful, imperfect human experience and smash Him into it.

Here again (v. 9), we see Christ spoken of as being "made perfect." This has been addressed in the comment under 2:11. Jesus Christ, through His Incarnation, was fitted to be 'Captain of our salvation.' This time He is being fitted to be our 'Great High Priest.' Remember the context. This is not speaking of Christ's inherent essence, but an office. Also, remember 'perfect' carries the meaning of bringing to completion or fitness. This passage is showing a parallel between the process by which Israel obtained their high priest and the way we obtained ours.

> *"Called of God an high priest after the*
> *order of Melchisedec. Of whom we have*

many things to say, and hard to be uttered, seeing ye are dull of hearing." vv. 10-11

We have been comparing Christ to Aaronic high priests, so you may wonder why the author has now, twice, brought up this 'Melchisedec.' This is because there are differences between that order and the Aaronic, or Levitical order. This will be treated much more fully under the comments on chapter 7, so we will defer as our author does, but for different reasons.

Notice, though, that the problem with getting the point across lay not with the messenger, or the subject matter, but with the hearer ("ye are dull of hearing"). A tool becomes dull from overuse without maintenance. These struggling Jewish converts seem to have heard these things enough to become complacent toward them. They knew so many things about the high priest and Melchisedec that they checked them off in their minds without considering the implications for their present situation. We, too, can become 'dull of hearing' if we are not careful. We may have the tendency to 'check out'- to think about something else- while the preacher is saying something we have heard before. In doing so, we close our ears to the Holy Spirit Who is trying to speak to us.

"For when for the time ye ought to be teachers, ye have need that one teach you again which be the first principles of the oracles of God; and are become such as have need of milk, and not of strong meat. For every one that useth milk is unskilful in the word of righteousness: for he is a babe.

But strong meat belongeth to them that are of full age, even those who by reason of use have their senses exercised to discern both good and evil." vv. 12-14

Christianity, per se, was new, but these people had grown up in the Old Testament. They had been taught by apostles. They, of all people, should have been firmly established in the faith. Milk is for those who have not reached a certain level of maturity. The author seems to be expressing frustration because his readers have a case of 'arrested development.' A 'spiritual babe' has not advanced beyond the basics, and is therefore unfit to face trial or persecution, much less to teach others in the way of doctrine. There are literally millions of videos on the internet of people who 'know who Melchisedec is,' and can tell you all about 'the Nephilim,' and what the Bible 'really' means, yet they haven't matured as Christians, if they have a profession at all. It doesn't take a solid Christian to make wild speculations on shrouded areas of the Bible. It takes a solid Christian to achieve what Paul exhorts:

"I therefore, the prisoner of the Lord, beseech you that ye walk worthy of the vocation wherewith ye are called, With all lowliness and meekness, with longsuffering, forbearing one another in love; Endeavouring to keep the unity of the Spirit in the bond of peace." Ephesians 4:1-3

Notice *"unskillful in the word of righteousness* (verse 13)." We learn the Bible, not for knowledge, not for 'views' or 'likes,' but that we may be able to disciple others. Notice also, "by reason of use." The senses are exercised when truths are received and applied, not ignored. The same stone can either sharpen or dull iron.

HEBREWS CHAPTER 6

"It is a great advantage for a system of philosophy to be substantially true." -George Santayana[83]

"Therefore leaving the principles of the doctrine of Christ, let us go on unto perfection;" Hebrews 6:1a

Don't let the chapter break between 5:14 and here interrupt the train of thought. Our first century Jewish Christians were just told they needed to be reminded of the 'first principles' of Christ. 6:1 is continuation of that admonition, with an encouragement to go on into 'perfection' or maturity. It is difficult to serve God properly when elementary doctrines such as eternal security are not settled in the believer's mind.

"not laying again the foundation of repentance from dead works, and of faith toward God, Of the doctrine of baptisms, and of laying on of hands, and of resurrection of the dead, and of eternal judgment." vv. 1b-2

The commentators have much to say regarding this list of doctrinal items, and one can easily get bogged down in them. There are attempts to break them down in different ways.

---

[83] Santayana, George *The Unknowable-Oxford Lectures on Philosophy 1910-1932* (Kessinger Whitefish, 1924), p. 4.

Some even think they aren't Christian ideas, but Judaic ones, and are therefore to be abandoned.[84]

The context seems to beg the consideration of these things as foundational for one leaving Judaism and being introduced into Christianity-in other words, the shadows are to be exchanged for the substance. Dead works (the rites[85] and sacrifices that foreshadowed Christ but could never truly 'make the comers thereunto perfect" [10:1]) were traded for Christ's perfect work. They have been settled, and it is time to build thereon. Answers to Old Testament questions, like resurrection of the dead, had been revealed.

This writer has noticed a possible parallel between the list in verses 1 and 2, and the list in verses 4 and 5. If such exists, this would bring further continuity between these verses which are so often taken in isolation.

---

[84] Such as Griffith Thomas, *Let Us Go On*, p. 71.

[85] There are at least three ways of interpreting 'baptisms' in this verse. It refers to (1) the washings that were required by the Law (Exodus 29:4 and 17, etc.), (2) the Christian baptisms that are taught in the New Testament (water baptism as a means of identification with Christ upon profession of faith, versus the baptism of the Holy Ghost at regeneration-there are many denominations who have still not understood this), or (3) the difference between the baptisms of John the Baptist and the Christian churches.

Repentance from dead works	Once enlightened
Faith toward God	Tasted of the heavenly gift
Doctrine of baptisms	Partakers of the Holy Ghost
Laying on of hands	Tasted of the good word of God
Resurrection and eternal judgment	The powers of the world to come

Indeed, it is critical to the proper understanding of the passage to *not* take it in isolation from its surrounding context.

"And this will we do, if God permit." v. 3

"This" is the going "on unto perfection" of verse 1. The "For" of the next verse is yet another link in this unbroken chain.

> *"For it is impossible for those who were once enlightened, and have tasted of the heavenly gift, and were made partakers of the Holy Ghost, And have tasted the good word of God, and the powers of the world to come, If they shall fall away, to renew them again unto repentance; seeing they crucify to themselves the Son of God afresh, and put him to an open shame."* vv. 4-6

This passage is notorious. It is so ominous in its perceived implications, that many avoid it altogether. Both G. Campbell Morgan and Alexander Maclaren pass it by without so much as a nod in their works on Hebrews.

One way of reaching a conclusion concerning its meaning is to make a determination on the salvific status of "those who were once enlightened." In other words, are these people saved or lost? If they are not truly saved, the problem vanishes. This view is held mainly by those influenced by Reformation era Calvinistic doctrine. Pink said, ". . .Calvinists have, generally, affirmed that this passage is treating of mere professors."[86] To help Pink establish his claim, we will bracket the entire history of Reformed doctrine as follows.

William Tyndale (c. 1494-1536) addressed this passage in the prologue to his translation of Hebrews:

> ". . .they which know the truth, and yet
> willingly refuse the light, and choose rather
> to dwell in darkness, and refuse Christ, . .
> .cannot be renewed, . . .to be converted:"[87]

John MacArthur holds the same view some 520 years later.

> "In that passage, the writer of Hebrews is
> speaking to the unsaved who have heard the
> truth and acknowledged it, but who have
> hesitated to embrace Christ. The Holy Spirit

---

[86] Pink, *Hebrews*, p. 403.
[87] Tyndale. William *Works of William Tyndale Volume I* (Banner of Truth Trust, 2010), p. 522.

warns them, 'You had better come to Christ now, for if you fall away it will be impossible for you to come again to the point of repentance.'"[88]

The opposing view is that they *were* saved but lost their salvation due to the 'falling away.' The writers above would be considered Calvinistic, while those who believe salvation can be forsaken and lost are generally considered Arminian. Any denomination that does not embrace the eternal security of the believer will fall on this side of the fence.

"Both Calvinist and Arminian have seemingly been convinced that this scripture sustains their peculiar belief."[89]

There exists a kind of hybrid approach which says that the dispensation (period of time in God's plan for the ages) one finds themselves in determines whether they can maintain their salvation or if it is upheld by God. It is held that since the book of Hebrews carries special significance for the Tribulation Jewish population (this writer agrees with this part only), and the Tribulation period is a different dispensation than the one in which eternal security is guaranteed,

---

[88] MacArthur, John, https://www.gty.org/library/questions/QA198/hebrews-6-and-the-loss-of-salvation, accessed 7-21-2023.

[89] Rowley, J.B. *Exposition of Hebrews Six "An Age-Long Battleground"* (Bibliotheca Sacra, July 1937, https://www.galaxie.com/article/bsac94-375-05) accessed 7-22-2023.

this passage speaks of those who can potentially lose their salvation (see Excursus 1).[90]

Another 'easy escape' is to make the passage hypothetical, in other words, this scenario would not take place in reality.

> "The things I have just pointed out are declared in our present Scripture to have been experiences of some who might fall away, and if they *did* fall away, it would be impossible for them to be renewed in repentance."[91]

Does this interpretation fall better on the ear? If it does, it is because it is far nearer the truth than the other interpretations that preceded it. The key to this passage does not lie in the spiritual *standing* of those described. The wrong focus has entered because the context of the passage was not maintained. The entire book of Hebrews is

---

[90] This position, called 'moderate dispensationalism' was pioneered by Dr. Peter S. Ruckman and can be found in his many works including his Hebrews and Revelation commentaries, and a book called *How to Teach Dispensational Truth* (all self-published). The latter sets the teaching out systematically. The majority of Dr. Ruckman's doctrinal positions were Biblically sound, but this one is not. It wrests the Scriptures in a way similar to that of hyper-Calvinism, where an idea foreign to the text is superimposed on the text, allowing the text to be removed from its context, and piled upon a man-made foundation. Remember, "A text without context is pretext."

[91] Greene, *Hebrews*, p. 223. See also Wuest, *Hebrews*, p. 117.

written to Christians,[92] therefore the question cannot be whether these people are saved; The author is exhorting saved people. Read the opening verses again. Notice "let us go on" . . . "this we will do if God permit" and "For." The author is driving a 'Christian living' bus, and if we switch to a 'salvation bus,' we won't end up where he was trying to take us. Stay with him through all the stops!

> "He did not say, "Do not go back into Judaism"-or into a life of pagan sin-with the idea of losing their redemption. It is a call to go on from where they are to what God wills them to be, **unto perfection.**"[93]

> "The whole tenor of the text reveals that he is speaking of *rewards* which are the result of salvation. In verse 6 he says, "If they shall fall away, to renew them to repentance"- not to salvation, but to *repentance*. . .So the writer of Hebrews is talking about the *fruit* of salvation. Not about the *root* of salvation."[94]

Look quickly at verse nine of our text: "But, beloved, we are persuaded better things of you, and **things that accompany salvation**, though

---

[92] There are those who say that the shift from "us" in verse 1 to "those" in verse 4 separates the saved from the unsaved. This does violence to the text. "Those," are clearly to be placed in apposition to "you" in verse 9.

[93] Hobbs, *Hebrews*, p. 56.

[94] McGee, J. Vernon *Thru the Bible – Vol. V* (Thomas Nelson, 1983), p. 546.

we thus speak." Things that accompany salvation, not salvation itself.

Chances are that this interpretation runs counter to what you've heard. Surely, we must do better than this if we are going to go against such a great cloud of witnesses, spanning hundreds of years! And what about this 'impossible?' Isn't God the 'God of second chances?'

Just like in every tricky passage we have encountered thus far, we will run through our imaginary checklist:

(1) What is the context?
(2) What does the passage actually say?
(3) What Old Testament parallel is the author of Hebrews trying to draw? [And for good measure let's add one more in]
(4) Are there any direct cross-references that are helpful?

The first two are done, so it is on to #3. The Old Testament parallel is still Kadesh Barnea (from Chapter 3: the failure to enter rest). Let's read from Numbers 14:7-10a.

> *"And Joshua the son of Nun, and Caleb the son of Jephunneh, which were of them that searched the land, rent their clothes: And they spake unto all the company of the children of Israel, saying, The land, which we passed through to search it, is an exceeding good land. If the LORD delight in us, then he will bring us into this land, and give it us; a land which floweth with milk and honey. Only rebel not ye*

against the LORD, neither fear ye the people of the land; for they are bread for us: their defence is departed from them, and the LORD is with us: fear them not. But all the congregation bade stone them with stones."

Israel not only refused to enter but wanted to return to Egypt. This refusal provoked God to express His intention to kill the Israelites and start over. Moses interceded on their behalf, which God honored. Yet He said in verses 22-23:

"Because all those men which have seen my glory, and my miracles, which I did in Egypt and in the wilderness, and have tempted me now these ten times, and have not hearkened to my voice; Surely they shall not see the land which I sware unto their fathers, neither shall any of them that provoked me see it:"

This is sounding quite a bit like our text in Hebrews 6. They saw the land. They tasted its fruit. They had God's promises. They refused. They wanted to go back. God brought them this far, but He would not take them any further-not because He didn't want to, but because of their refusal to obey a direct order.

What about the impossibility of repentance? Look down at verse 40-45:

"And they rose up early in the morning, and gat them up into the top of the mountain, saying, Lo, we be here, and will go up unto the place which the LORD hath

promised: for we have sinned. And Moses said, Wherefore now do ye transgress the commandment of the LORD? but it shall not prosper. Go not up, for the LORD is not among you; that ye be not smitten before your enemies. For the Amalekites and the Canaanites are there before you, and ye shall fall by the sword: because ye are turned away from the LORD, therefore the LORD will not be with you. But they presumed to go up unto the hill top: nevertheless the ark of the covenant of the LORD, and Moses, departed not out of the camp. Then the Amalekites came down, and the Canaanites which dwelt in that hill, and smote them, and discomfited them, even unto Hormah."

They were not allowed to return to Egypt, and they could not claim inheritance. We have already discussed these parallels and how they relate to our Christian experience. Think also of Israel as a nation when they rejected Jesus as Messiah. Once this happened, there was no going back to the blessings of having accepted Him. Many Jews were saved during and after (Acts 2), but the program changed, and God went a different way (Romans 11:11).

What about a cross reference for this idea? Was there someone else who despised an inheritance that was due to them and could not repent and reclaim it? Check Hebrews 12:16-17.

> *"Lest there be any fornicator, or profane person, as Esau, who for one morsel of meat sold his birthright. For ye know how that afterward, when he would have inherited the blessing, he was rejected: for he found no place of repentance, though he sought it carefully with tears."*

This is a reference to Genesis 25. Esau lost his inheritance as Isaac's firstborn. Once he gave it up, he could not get it back. Again, this isn't a salvation issue! This writer is convinced that it is in the Bible to show how when one yields to the flesh, he may lose an eternal reward. Bob Jones Sr. said,

> "Never sacrifice the *permanent* on the altar of the *immediate*."

For our first century Hebrew Christians, they, like their forefathers, were given a command. Their forefathers were told to go in, they were told to stay out. It was a direct order. Those that disobeyed at Kadesh Barnea died in the wilderness with no inheritance. Those who returned to Jerusalem and to Judaism (if any did) were burned in the siege of Titus. We have been given a direct order. We are to take up our cross and follow Him. We are to be fishers of men-to fulfill the Great Commission. If we refuse in favor of serving the flesh, it is as good as crucifying Him to ourselves. Either we are on the cross (living the crucified life) or He is.

> "We want to be saved, but we insist that Christ do all the dying. We remain king within the little kingdom of Mansoul and wear our

tinsel crown with all the pride of a Caesar, but we doom ourselves to shadows and weakness and spiritual sterility."[95]

"The end result insofar as their lives are concerned, as well as the lost souls to whom they do not witness, is to negate God's redemptive purpose. Thus they join with the crucifiers. God's purpose goes on in another place, another time. But, for the rebels, their opportunity is lost forever."[96]

Doesn't it make far more sense to exhort the readers of Hebrews in this way? Those who are saved are kept by God; what they need is to be careful to maintain good works (Titus 3:8). Christian, it is time to settle in your heart, once and for all, the matter of eternal security. If you spend all your time worried about whether you are saved or not, you won't have any left to worry about whether your neighbor is saved or not. Please be encouraged to follow God's general command to evangelize the lost and be especially sensitive to the Spirit when He places a distinct burden on your heart for something He wants you to do, or someone He wants you to reach. There is a reward to be gained by obedience, and there is the possibility of irrevocable loss by disobedience.

> *"For the earth which drinketh in the rain that cometh oft upon it, and bringeth forth herbs meet for them by whom it is*

---

[95] Tozer, A.W. *A.W. Tozer: An Anthology* (Christian Publications 1984), p. 53.
[96] Hobbs *Hebrews*, p. 61.

dressed, receiveth blessing from God: But that which beareth thorns and briers is rejected, and is nigh unto cursing; whose end is to be burned." vv. 7-8

These two verses are put often forth as confirming the interpretation that Hebrews 6 is about salvation, and not maturity. For example:

"That there were two classes of people, one lost and one saved, who alike had been enlightened by the Word, *is confirmed in the parable given in verses 7 and 8* (emphasis mine)."[97]

They are also claimed to enforce the possibility of a loss of salvation. But is this true? At this point, those who hold the former view go off into a discourse on a different subject (heaven and hell, the fear of God, soul-winning, etc.), and those who hold the latter view take the opportunity to discourse upon their pet doctrine. In other words, they deviate from the subject, taking the mind of the reader to some other place than where the author (or Author) intended. If we are trying to find out what this book is saying, we should stay in context, and see how the Bible treats the subject at hand. We will view this passage in the light of Scripture. Wouldn't you rather the Holy Ghost be your guide than some axe grinder?

Our passage is an illustration that mentions (1) earth, (2) rain, (3) herbs, (4) those for whom it is dressed, (5) receiving blessings from God, (6)

---

[97] Greene, *Hebrews*, p. 232-233.

thorns and briers (7) rejection, (8) nigh unto cursing, and (9) burning.

So far, the Bible itself has guided us to a proper interpretation and will continue to do so. Continuing that pattern, let's find another passage (or two) that actually complements the one under consideration. Jesus gave a similar parable in Matthew 13 and Mark 4. Mark's account runs as follows:

> *"Hearken; Behold, there went out a sower to sow: And it came to pass, as he sowed, some fell by the way side, and the fowls of the air came and devoured it up. And some fell on stony ground, where it had not much earth; and immediately it sprang up, because it had no depth of earth: But when the sun was up, it was scorched; and because it had no root, it withered away. And some fell among thorns, and the thorns grew up, and choked it, and it yielded no fruit. And other fell on good ground, and did yield fruit that sprang up and increased; and brought forth, some thirty, and some sixty, and some an hundred."* Mark 4:3-8

Happily, we are not left to decipher the meaning of the parable. Christ lays it out for His disciples, who pass it on to us:

> *"The sower soweth the word. And these are they by the way side, where the word is sown; but when they have heard, Satan cometh immediately, and taketh away the word that was sown in their hearts. And*

these are they likewise which are sown on stony ground; who, when they have heard the word, immediately receive it with gladness; And have no root in themselves, and so endure but for a time: afterward, when affliction or persecution ariseth for the word's sake, immediately they are offended. And these are they which are sown among thorns; such as hear the word, And the cares of this world, and the deceitfulness of riches, and the lusts of other things entering in, choke the word, and it becometh unfruitful. And these are they which are sown on good ground; such as hear the word, and receive it, and bring forth fruit, some thirtyfold, some sixty, and some an hundred." Mark 4:14-20

So, the seed that is sown is the Word of God. The Sower is obviously God, though He works through human agency. According to verse 15, the ground is the heart of the hearers. It is possible, according to verses 18 and 19, for some ground to produce thorns. The emphasis of the parable comes in at the end of verse 19 through verse 20. It is <u>fruitfulness</u>.[98] Too many are looking to

---

[98] An example of inconsistent interpretation is found in a sizeable tome by a respected modern author. In *Interpreting the Parables* (InterVarsity Press, Second Edition 2012), p. 291, Blomberg rightly says the parable is about spiritual fruit-bearing. On the very next page, he claims the unfruitful plants spring from those who "respond to the word with less than saving faith. This shifts not only the focus of the parable mid-stream, but the target audience. Quite sloppy speechmaking for One Who made no mistakes! The seed produces nothing in the life of the unbeliever.

interpret who is saved and lost by the fruit, and not the condition of the soil.

> "The difference was in neither the sower nor the seed, but the soils."[99]

The effectiveness of God's word in your life will be determined by the condition of your heart. God has done everything it takes to facilitate growth and abundance. You are responsible for the condition of your heart. It is impossible to go through life without getting stepped on by someone. Will you let it make you hard? Will you distance yourself from people to the point where you find yourself on the wayside? Will you let the cares of this life weigh you down like the stones in this parable? Some people are such slaves to pleasure that they continue to add 'toys' to their lives beyond the point of their ability to care for them without impeding their service for God. Some develop no root. They may be saved, but they never anchor themselves in the word of God. How is your soil doing?

The author of Hebrews picks up the story *after the seed is sown* and is addressing what the ground (the heart of the believer) is producing! If we are being Biblically consistent, the context is indeed maturity, and not at all salvation.

We have unlocked what the earth/ground is, and discovered that fruit is what is desired, and thorns are not. In every instance, the *fruit production* is what is affected. Fruit is the good

---

[99] Hobbs, *Hebrews*, p. 62.

works God desires from those whom He has 'dressed.' In Isaiah 5, God has Isaiah tell another parable. It goes like this:

> *"And now, O inhabitants of Jerusalem, and men of Judah, judge, I pray you, betwixt me and my vineyard. What could have been done more to my vineyard, that I have not done in it? wherefore, when I looked that it should bring forth grapes, brought it forth wild grapes? And now go to; I will tell you what I will do to my vineyard: I will take away the hedge thereof, and it shall be eaten up; and break down the wall thereof, and it shall be trodden down: And I will lay it waste: it shall not be pruned, nor digged; but there shall come up briers and thorns: I will also command the clouds that they rain no rain upon it. For the vineyard of the LORD of hosts is the house of Israel..."*
> Isaiah 5:3-7a

Thorns are undesired fruit. They are the result of sin—of choosing of one's own way over God's way. Think about Adam. He chose his wife over God and thorns were the result. Israel chose their lucrative religious system over Christ and put thorns on His head. They can also spring up out of neglect (Proverbs 24:30-31). In the hand of a faithful messenger, they can teach you a lesson (Judges 8:16)!

Rain is God's blessing and is also connected with fruit bearing. God, at various times, withheld rain (I Kings 8:35). Israel's covenant with God included a promise of rain if they remained faithful, and drought if they did not (Deuteronomy 11:17). Two things are required for crops to grow: you must plant them, then you must water them. Paul says this in I Corinthians 3:6, "I have planted, Apollos watered; but God gave the increase." The seeding is the initial giving of God's word, the watering occurs afterward. Everything that is listed in our text occurs after this and helps us place our parable into a post-salvation context.

What about the 'cursing'? In Mark 11, Jesus inspects a fig tree. He has every reason to expect fruit, yet He finds none. He curses the tree, and it withers, never to produce fruit again (a 'withered hand' can do no work). In the next scene, Jesus is clearing out the Temple (vv. 15-19), and when they return, they pass the same fig tree. Jesus came and inspected the Temple, and found His people producing bad fruit, and He 'cleaned house.'

What about the 'burning'? Let's go back to I Corinthians 3. After saying he planted and Apollos watered, Paul expounds further:

> *"So then neither is he that planteth any thing, neither he that watereth; but God that giveth the increase. Now he that planteth and he that watereth are one: and every man shall receive his own reward according to his own labour. For we are labourers together with God: ye are God's husbandry, ye are God's building. According to the grace of God which is given unto me, as a wise masterbuilder, I have laid the foundation, and another buildeth thereon.*

But let every man take heed how he buildeth thereupon. For other foundation can no man lay than that is laid, which is Jesus Christ. Now if any man build upon this foundation gold, silver, precious stones, wood, hay, stubble; Every man's work shall be made manifest: for the day shall declare it, because it shall be revealed by fire; and the fire shall try every man's work of what sort it is. If any man's work abide which he hath built thereupon, he shall receive a reward. If any man's work shall be burned, he shall suffer loss: but he himself shall be saved; yet so as by fire." I Corinthians 3:7-15

Look at Isaiah 10:17 as well:

"And the light of Israel shall be for a fire, and his Holy One for a flame: and it shall burn and devour his thorns and his briers in one day;"

That 'one day' is the coming day of Judgment. In that day, our <u>works</u> will be put to the flame, and only what was done for Christ will survive. God help us that we will have something to show for the years and years of blessing God has rained upon us.

"But, beloved, we are persuaded better things of you, and things that accompany salvation, though we thus speak. For God is not unrighteous to forget your work and labour of love, which ye have shewed toward his name, in that ye have ministered to the saints, and do minister. And

we desire that every one of you do shew the same diligence to the full assurance of hope unto the end: That ye be not slothful, but followers of them who through faith and patience inherit the promises." vv. 9-12

Again, we are discussing "Things that *accompany* salvation" and not salvation itself. Some things that accompany salvation are then listed, and assurance is given that these things will not be forgotten. If someone had done these things which accompanied their salvation, then became unsaved, how can it be said that God would not forget that work? For Him to do so would be unrighteous, according to this passage. It becomes increasingly ridiculous that this passage can be used to teach a loss of salvation! After giving assurance that God will honor their good fruit, the author exhorts his readers to match their continued diligence to that assurance. This is followed by a mention of the inheritance of promises. Every last word fits into a spiritual maturity context.

"God is not unrighteous to forget what Christ has done (v. 6), and in like manner, He is not unrighteous to forget what Christians have done (v. 10)"[100]

"For when God made promise to Abraham, because he could swear by no greater, he sware by himself, Saying, Surely blessing I will bless thee, and multiplying I will multiply thee. And so, after he had

---

[100] Griffith Thomas, *Go On*, p. 76.

patiently endured, he obtained the promise. For men verily swear by the greater: and an oath for confirmation is to them an end of all strife. Wherein God, willing more abundantly to shew unto the heirs of promise the immutability of his counsel, confirmed it by an oath: That by two immutable things, in which it was impossible for God to lie, we might have a strong consolation, who have fled for refuge to lay hold upon the hope set before us: Which hope we have as an anchor of the soul, both sure and stedfast," vv. 13-19a

The author goes from assurance to assurance and places his statements firmly on an Old Testament foundation. This passage refers to the promise God made Abraham in Genesis chapter 12, confirmed in chapter 17, and finally began to be fulfilled in chapter 21, when Isaac is born. God confirmed it once again in chapter 22:16-17. Abraham waited about 40 years from the first promise to the first fulfillment.

Men often make covenants flippantly, or else change their minds later and push the boundaries of the agreement. To settle disputes, they appeal to an arbiter-one 'greater than themselves.' There is no higher court, no greater Arbiter than the Lord Himself, the just Judge, Who knows all and can never lie. Because He has sworn on Himself, we will live as long as He lives. Look at the terminology here: promise and immutability, confirmed, consolation, hope, anchor, sure, stedfast. . .does any of this sound like someone who is in danger of losing their salvation?

Notice *"we. . .who have fled for refuge."* The mind of a Hebrew Christian would immediately flash to what we now call Numbers 35.

> *"And the LORD spake unto Moses, saying, Speak unto the children of Israel, and say unto them, When ye be come over Jordan into the land of Canaan; Then ye shall appoint you cities to be cities of refuge for you; that the slayer may flee thither, which killeth any person at unawares. And they shall be unto you cities for refuge from the avenger; that the manslayer die not, until he stand before the congregation in judgment."* Numbers 35:9-12.

Each of us is guilty of the death of someone. "How?" you ask. It was our sin that made Christ's death necessary. That is why *"The wages of sin is death."* (Romans 6:23). We who are saved have fled to Christ for refuge and will be preserved until judgment. Look at verse 25 of the same chapter: *"and he shall abide in it unto the death of the high priest, which was anointed with the holy oil."* We are safe for as long as our High Priest lives!

> *"and which entereth into that within the veil; Whither the forerunner is for us entered, even Jesus, made an high priest for ever after the order of Melchisedec."* v. 19b-20

We have now come to the crux of this great book, and that is the superiority of Christ's priesthood. It excels all others in efficacy, duration, depth, dependability, width, wonder, and majesty. It is effective for any man, woman, or child anywhere. It is unending and thorough, saving 'to the uttermost' as we shall see shortly. Because Jesus Christ kept His promise to God the Father in going through the death of the cross, God the Father will keep His promise to God the Son that He will redeem us; and the text is clear-God <u>cannot</u> lie.

At the heels of this promise (6:18-19) comes the return to a theme that has only been mentioned in passing (5:6, 5:10), the priesthood 'after the order of Melchisedec.'

The author of Hebrews will now seek to prove the nature and superiority of Christ's priesthood by comparing it with Melchizedec's.

HEBREWS CHAPTER 7

"My interest was fanned by two coincidences-the kind of coincidences that cause and effect just can't allow, but which seem to happen all the same in the world of unchangeable events." -James Blish[101]

"For this Melchisedec, king of Salem, priest of the most high God, who met Abraham returning from the slaughter of the kings, and blessed him; To whom also Abraham gave a tenth part of all; first being by interpretation King of righteousness, and after that also King of Salem, which is, King of peace; Without father, without mother, without descent, having neither beginning of days, nor end of life; but made like unto the Son of God; abideth a priest continually." Hebrews 7:1-3

The story of Melchizedek is found in Genesis 14, and his billing is limited to a mere 3 verses (18-20). There has been much speculation as to the identity of this man Melchisedec. There is the Hebrew tradition that he was Shem,[102] who was still alive in Abraham's day, and in which case 'Melchizedek' would be a title. Some say Job.[103]

---

[101] From *The Quincunx of Time*, quoted in Clegg, Brian *The God Effect* (St. Martin's Press, New York, 2006), p. 116.

[102] Morris, Henry *The Genesis Record* (Baker Book House, 1976), 320. (These men did not necessarily believe any of these guesses; these footnotes indicate only where the references were found.)

[103] Ironside, *Hebrews and Titus*, p. 85.

Some say Cheops[104] or Philitis,[105] which are both given credit as builders of the Great Pyramid of Egypt. Some have even claimed that he was "the 'unfallen Adam' from some other planet, sent to this planet to observe the progress of God's redemption for the fallen race of our Adam"[106] This is silly of course. Two more possibilities exist, the first of which is that Melchisedek was an appearance of the preincarnate Christ.[107] The final being that he was simply a man named Melchizedek who happened to be both king of Salem and priest of God at the time. Arguing identity, however, falls outside of the point the author of Hebrews is trying to make. What we are being asked to consider is the *priestly order* that is or is typical of the order of Christ's priesthood. What is meant by that statement is that either there is an eternal order to which both Melchizedek and Christ belonged, or that Christ's priesthood displays parallels with that of Melchizedek. As you may have noticed, the description of Melchizedek in our text is less than clear when describing him, and the eternal nature of the priesthood is just as ambiguous. If you take him to be Christ Himself, then the Melchizedekian order *must* be eternal in both directions, with Christ performing literal priestly duties in the days of Abraham, for that is

---

[104] Ibid.

[105] Lockyer, Herbert *All the Men of the Bible* (Zondervan Publishing House, 1975), p. 235.

[106] Morris, *Genesis*, p. 320.

[107] This idea is given fair treatment in Henry Morris' *The Genesis Record* based on textual grounds, with objections answered. He expresses no dogmatism.

what Melchizedek did. If not, does the priestly order extend in only the direction of eternity future, beginning with Christ's incarnation and moving forward? These are great questions and well worth one's time to ponder. When considering this section, we will compare the priesthoods and get the author's point in mentioning them.

> "We think of the word "order" as denoting inheritance, or succession; but here it denotes character of being, and office."[108]

The Melchisedekian side of the coin is described directly in vv. 1-3 (king and priest, without descent, etc.). Here are some more parallels that are less obvious from the text:

(1)   Melchizedek's order existed outside the law. Moses and the law would come much later, after the sojourn in Egypt. This means that unlike the Levitical priests, Melchizedek did not mediate the law. Christ mediates not the law, but grace. Consider Galatians 3:19:

> *"Wherefore then serveth the law? It was added because of transgressions, till the seed should come to whom the promise was made; and it was ordained by angels in the hand of a mediator."*

(2)   Melchizedek's order existed outside the nation of Israel. Abraham is the father of the nation that would become Israel. At the time of Melchizedek, no 'Israel' existed as a people. The Levites served only Israel.

---

[108] Newell, *Hebrews*, p. 211.

Christ's priesthood is open to and effective for anyone, without deference to ethnicity, nationality, or geography.

(3)   Melchizedek and Christ serve(d) as mediators.

(4)   Both hold/held offices of priest and king. Their titles are very similar.

(5)   Both receive(d) tithes.

(6)   Both have/had an association with bread and wine.

(7)   As dealt with by the texts, both ministries are described *following* the redemption of people. When we read about Melchizedek in Genesis 14, he doesn't show up until after the battle and rescue. The ministry of Christ is here described according to what it offers to saved people. (As stated under the comments on 4:14, the Levitical priesthood served people that were already redeemed. See how precisely the Bible keeps its types? Hebrews takes for granted that its audience is a saved group of people!)

(8)   As dealt with by the texts, their ministry is one of comfort and help, not of sacrificing for sins.[109] This is related to the last point. Melchizedek did not come with sheep for slaughter, but with bread and wine.

---

[109] This is not to say that Melchisedek did not offer sacrifices. It is evident that the primary mission of both was sacrifice-Christ's atoning work in parallel with the implied sacrifices of Melchizedek.

(It may be objected that this episode comes before the great 'salvation' passage of Genesis 15, but this is answered by the fact that Abraham's dealings with God precede both, that Genesis 15 has everything to do with the promise of inheritance, and not with Abraham's individual soul, and that Christ's Passover meal-the first 'communion'-preceded His death and resurrection. The Passover that it typified also preceded the sin offerings of the law of Moses. We must be careful in how we apply these typologies. Genesis 15 is rightly used to illustrate that Abraham's righteousness came through belief. Paul did so in Romans 4. But Abraham did not get 'saved' in Genesis 15; he believed and followed God long before that).

"Now consider how great this man was, unto whom even the patriarch Abraham gave the tenth of the spoils. And verily they that are of the sons of Levi, who receive the office of the priesthood, have a commandment to take tithes of the people according to the law, that is, of their brethren, though they come out of the loins of Abraham: But he whose descent is not counted from them received tithes of Abraham, and blessed him that had the promises. And without all contradiction the less is blessed of the better. And here men that die receive tithes; but there he receiveth them, of whom it is witnessed that he liveth. And as I may so say, Levi also, who

receiveth tithes, payed tithes in Abraham. For he was yet in the loins of his father, when Melchisedec met him." vv. 4-10

Now here is the point of this passage. This argument should serve as proof to the Jewish believers from the Scripture that Christ supersedes Abraham, as well as the entire Levitical priesthood! He does this by first proving that Melchizedek was better than Abraham. It is of note that the idea of a 'tithe' is established prior to the giving of the Law (this has implications for those who use the annulling of the Law as an excuse not to tithe). Then, since Levi is 'in the loins' of Abraham (that Abraham was greater than any living Jew would be uncontroversial), Levi is considered to have given tithes to Melchizedek as well.

"If therefore perfection were by the Levitical priesthood, (for under it the people received the law,) what further need was there that another priest should rise after the order of Melchisedec, and not be called after the order of Aaron? For the priesthood being changed, there is made of necessity a change also of the law." vv. 11-12

Verses like these should serve as a death blow to theories which claim that during the tribulation period, the Jewish people will return to the Old Testament priesthood by order of God. They will return, but not at God's hand. Their religion will be just as unacceptable to God as it was the day Christ died. To say they return to that old dispensation is to say that Christ's work can be undone-that His fulfilling of the law didn't happen, and, for our present purposes, His priesthood is suspended. It simply cannot be. The law was imperfect (*"For what the law could not do, in that it was weak through the flesh, God sending his own Son in the likeness of sinful flesh, and for sin, condemned sin in the flesh:"* Romans 8:3), and according to our text, the Levitical priesthood was imperfect, and they were inexorably linked together.

Note that verse 12 contains the first allusion to Christ since the end of chapter 6. The author does not actually start putting Christ and Melchizedek together until now.

> *"For he of whom these things are spoken pertaineth to another tribe, of which no man gave attendance at the altar. For it is evident that our Lord sprang out of Juda; of which tribe Moses spake nothing concerning priesthood. And it is yet far more evident: for that after the similitude of Melchisedec there ariseth another priest, Who is made, not after the law of a carnal commandment, but after the power of an endless life."* vv. 13-16

Melchizedek sprang from no Jewish tribe, for he lived before there was such a thing. Christ is also of a different order for the fact that He (at least as far as His earthly parents were concerned) sprang from a tribe other than Levi, from which the priests were to be selected. It is from the line of Judah that the *kings* of Israel descended (at least originally). Looking back on Israel's history, we see two threads-one of priest, and one of king- running in parallel. The priesthood was established by Moses, and the kingship was added by Samuel. The attempted mixing of the two brought judgment (Saul in I Samuel 13:8-14, and Uzziah in II Chronicles 26:16-21), for there was only to be One Who could hold both offices.[110] That Priest-King holds His office through the "power of an endless life." Hallelujah!

Wouldn't it be fitting for a king from the line of Judah to weigh in on the necessity of a Melchizedekian Priest? Look at the next verse:

> *"For he testifieth, Thou art a priest for*
> *ever after the order of Melchisedec."* v. 17

At this point the author quotes yet another Psalm-this time Psalm 110:4. J. R. Church wrote a book entitled "Hidden Prophecies in the Psalms." His entry on this Psalm is so startling, so beautiful that this writer will reproduce the greater part of it here.

> "Psalm 110 declares the coming of Christ to establish His kingdom. Verse one refers to the past 2,000 intervening years between His First Coming and His Second Coming. Christ has been in heaven at the right hand of the Father… This (vv. 2,4-6) is a picture of Armageddon when the Savior comes to deliver Israel and destroy the antichrist. Not only will Christ become the King of kings and

---

[110] We see what a mess is made in history when the Church meddles in the government and vice-versa. People will die.

Lord of lords, He will also reveal His priesthood. He is the altogether unique High Priest established, not after the order of the Levitical priesthood, but after the order of Melchisedek. This is most important in relation to Israel. The Levitical priesthood was uniquely Jewish. On the other hand, the priesthood of Melchizedek represented an all-encompassing order of worship. Here enters the legitimate claim of Gentile New Testament Christianity found right here in the middle of a Jewish book! This one little verse (v. 4) represents a proverbial bomb in the midst of an exclusive Judaism. Christ is High Priest of all!"

"The religious Jew emphatically denies the legitimacy of Gentile Christianity. He denies the authority of Jesus Christ as the Messiah of Israel and the Savior of the rest of the world. As this dispensation closes, however, the religious Jewish community will recognize our claim to Jesus Christ! The New Testament book of Hebrews contains an explanation for the Chosen People. Being the 19th book of the New Testament, like its counterpart, the Psalm (19th book of the Old Testament), the treatise to the Hebrews is actually a message based on the Psalms. It is as if the treatise was written for Israel in this generation!"[111]

---

[111] Church, J.R. *Hidden Prophecies in the Psalms* (Prophecy Publications, 1986), p. 314-315.

"For there is verily a disannulling of the commandment going before for the weakness and unprofitableness thereof. For the law made nothing perfect, but the bringing in of a better hope did; by the which we draw nigh unto God." vv. 18-19

Here again we see that Hebrews concerns sanctification, for the purpose of the priesthood was to stand between man and God and bring them together. The law was made for a redeemed people, and the Levitical priesthood mediated the law for the purpose of sanctifying those people. According to this verse the commandment, or the law, made nothing perfect. In Melchizedek we have the hope of a better priesthood that does what the law could never do.

There are several ways in which the law was weak and/or unprofitable.

(1) <u>The law could not be kept perfectly because men are imperfect.</u>

"For what the law could not do, in that it was weak through the flesh, God sending his own Son in the likeness of sinful flesh, and for sin, condemned sin in the flesh:" Romans 8:13

(2) <u>The law could be kept externally, while the adherent remained rebellious internally.</u>

"Wherefore the Lord said, Forasmuch as this people draw near me with their mouth, and with their lips do honour me, but

have removed their heart far from me, and their fear toward me is taught by the precept of men:" Isaiah 29:13

(2)   <u>The law was only a foreshadow of the substance that would be brought in Christ.</u>

> *"For the law having a shadow of good things to come, and not the very image of the things, can never with those sacrifices which they offered year by year continually make the comers thereunto perfect."* Hebrews 10:1

Jesus Christ, our great High Priest is our hope, and it is by Him that we are able to draw nigh unto God. He is the 'daysman' sought by Job in Job 9:33. Hear John in I John 2:1:

> *"My little children, these things write I unto you, that ye sin not. And if any man sin, we have an advocate with the Father, Jesus Christ the righteous:"*

Notice also that Melchizedek, representing this hope, came before the law was ever instituted, thus displaying God's wisdom. God did not institute the law with the hope that man would keep it, then resign Himself to figuring out a 'plan B.'[112]

---

[112] We hold that God is omniscient, and therefore cannot act arbitrarily. There *must* be divine impetus for every action He undertakes. This begs the question of why He would design His redemptive history in such a way. Why do we have all this backstory? Why pull one man (Abraham) out from amongst all others? Why a chosen nation? Why not come to earth and redeem mankind immediately subsequent to the fall? Why the 'dispensations?' The answer is that

> *"And inasmuch as not without an oath he was made priest: (For those priests were made without an oath; but this with an oath by him that said unto him, The Lord sware and will not repent, Thou art a priest for ever after the order of Melchisedec:)"* vv. 20-21

In the Old Testament system there was no oath. If you were a Levite, you were a priest. When your number came up, you donned your accoutrements and took your turn. Yet there was an agreement before time began between the Father and the Son that He would serve as this great Mediator, for which the old law and old priesthood were but a shadow.

> "Jehovah sware, and will not change (H)is mind. His appointment is final, absolute, immutable. It can never be superseded, as that of Aaron has been. Heaven and earth may pass away, but it will not pass away."[113]

> *"By so much was Jesus made a surety of a better testament."* v. 22

This 'testament' is the agreement between God and us, that we can draw nigh to Him because of what Christ in His death has done. Christ did His

---

anything God does *must* be the best possible course of action because He is not only omniscient, but good. To do less than the best would be sin for God as well as man, and He can have no sin in Him. When confronted with divergent theological viewpoints concerning God's providence in human history, this axiom is foundational. It will help keep the student from making doctrinal errors.

[113] Meyer, *Holiest*, p. 95.

part on the cross, and we are invited to do ours when we hear the Gospel. It was agreed upon between the Father and His Son in the oath referred to in the previous verse. (It is not the *New Testament*. Our *New Testament* is a record of the institution and progress of the testament spoken here, just as the *Old Testament* is the history of the testament God placed man under before Christ's death.)

The Greek word for 'testament' here is the same word translated 'covenant' elsewhere. There is a difference between the two, and it is great wisdom (or Holy Spirit guidance) that caused our translators to choose one over the other. Every other translation places 'covenant' here. We will find out why 'testament' is correct in the comments under chapter 9.

> *"And they truly were many priests, because they were not suffered to continue by reason of death: But this man, because he continueth ever, hath an unchangeable priesthood. Wherefore he is able also to save them to the uttermost that come unto God by him, seeing he ever liveth to make intercession for them."* vv. 23-25

Verses 23 and 24 are straightforward. Christ's superiority is seen in that He will never die. His priesthood will ever continue, and is unchangeable, meaning it is dependable and consistent. We in America have a change in the presidency every four to eight years, and people and especially businesses undergo great trepidation worrying about what changes may be made and how it will affect them. With Christ there is no shadow of turning. His goodness is guaranteed, and His power to keep us cannot fail.

Because of His supreme superiority to the old priesthood, and His position as our great High Priest, He is able to see our salvation through all the way to glorification!

> "This ability of Christ is a truth of great importance, and one that is at the base of everything in our Christian life and experience. It is probably on this account that we find it so prominently set forth in the New Testament. "God is able to make him stand (Rom. 14:4); "able to stablish you" (Rom. 16:25); "able to keep you from falling, and to present you faultless" (Jude 24); "able to make all grace abound toward you" (II Cor. 9:8); "able to keep" (II Tim. 1:12); "able to build you up" (Acts 20:32); "able even to subdue" (Phil. 3:21); "able to do exceedingly abundantly above all that we ask or think" (Eph. 3:20). The more we are occupied with the power of the living Christ, the fuller, deeper, and richer our spiritual life will become."[114]

To this grand statement we dare add only the Scripture:

> *"Who hath saved us, and called us with an holy calling, not according to our works, but according to his own purpose and*

---

[114] Griffith Thomas, *Go On*, pp. 92-93.

grace, which was given us in Christ Jesus before the world began, But is now made manifest by the appearing of our Saviour Jesus Christ, who hath abolished death, and hath brought life and immortality to light through the gospel: Whereunto I am appointed a preacher, and an apostle, and a teacher of the Gentiles. For the which cause I also suffer these things: nevertheless I am not ashamed: for I know whom I have believed, and am persuaded that he is able to keep that which I have committed unto him against that day." II Timothy 1:9-12

"For such an high priest became us, who is holy, harmless, undefiled, separate from sinners, and made higher than the heavens; v. 26

We have followed others in assigning the meaning of "became" as 'being fit for.'[115] In time past a lady may complement another by saying something like "That dress is very becoming of you." She means a dress of such beauty is fitting for someone so pretty. Yet this verse is like 2:10 in that the author is showing the *contrast* between the things that are 'fit' together. In 2:10, the contrast was between the Creator of heaven and earth, and the lowliness of His task in condescending to us and suffering for us. Here, in 7:26, we see His perfect holiness and the extreme dignity of His office in contrast to "us," for whom

---

[115] For example, Wuest, *Hebrews,* p. 59, under his comments on Hebrews 2:10.

the author rightly leaves off describing in the same sentence.

> "Dr. Saphir calls attention to two things in this chapter: how much saving we need, and how well Christ can do it. His mediation must go low enough to reach the Cross, high enough to reach to heaven, and deep enough to enter into and abide in our hearts (Saphir, *Hebrews,* vol. i, p. 413-415). And so Christ on the Cross guarantees peace of conscience, while Christ on the Throne gives peace of heart. His death cancels our condemnation, and His life guarantees our access to the very presence of God.[116]

> *"Who needeth not daily, as those high priests, to offer up sacrifice, first for his own sins, and then for the people's: for this he did once, when he offered up himself."* v. 27

This idea has been discussed but is apt for completing the thought of the chapter: The finality of Christ's sacrifice. "he did this once" refers only to the offering up of a sacrifice for the people, not for Himself. He encompasses all that the old system foreshadowed. He is the Priest, the Sacrifice, the Temple, the Shewbread, the Lamp, the Laver, and the object of all its worship!

The need for a daily service, a repeated sacrifice is also evidence of the weakness and unprofitableness discussed above (verse 18).

---

[116] Griffith Thomas, *Go On,* p. 99.

"For the law maketh men high priests which have infirmity; but the word of the oath, which was since the law, maketh the Son, who is consecrated for evermore."

The law was instituted to help control the flesh (Galatians 3:19). God wanted those who looked on Israel's peculiar worship to extrapolate His holiness from the conduct of His chosen people. Because of man's weakness, and often his frank rebellion, he could never be a perfect high priest. Christ's oath transcends the law and is what made Him our High Priest. God's promise will never fail, and is not dependent on any man's imperfection, certainly not our own.

HEBREWS CHAPTER 8

"However much you rail against the customs of Arthur's court, you shall not enter until I have gone inside and spoken with Arthur" – Glewlwyd Gafaelfawr[117]

> *"Now of the things which we have spoken this is the sum: We have such an high priest, who is set on the right hand of the throne of the Majesty in the heavens; A minister of the sanctuary, and of the true tabernacle, which the Lord pitched, and not man. For every high priest is ordained to offer gifts and sacrifices: wherefore it is of necessity that this man have somewhat also to offer."* Hebrews 8:1-3

We have reached the apex of the Epistle to the Hebrews. Our author has been at pains to show how Christ is superior in every way to every bastion of Judaic faith and hope, and now arrives at the most important aspect of Christ for the Jewish Christians to which he writes. All the theological claims and exhortations to faithfulness and maturity hinge on the current office Christ holds as high Priest. It is Christ's work as high Priest that accomplishes everything that the law, the sacrifices, the tabernacle, and the temple could only point to.

"Hitherto we have been considering the Person of the Priest. Now we are to consider

------

[117] Gantz, Jeffrey, trans. *The Mabinogion* (Barnes & Noble, 1996), p. 138.

His Work, and see that as priest He perfectly discharges the duties of His office. Melchizedek is used to set forth the Person of the priest, and Aaron to set forth His Work."[118]

Notice that Christ 'is set on the right hand of the throne' and does not sit upon it. This is indicative of His current office of High Priest, not His future office of King.

"The throne He occupies and from which He ministers is not David's throne, which He will one day occupy here on earth as the promised Messiah (Matt. 25:31). Rather, He was identified with the throne of 'the Majesty in the heavens.' The authority assigned to the One so enthroned was to be 'a minister of the sanctuary and of the true tabernacle.' (Heb. 8:2). Thus, He was not appointed to be a king in an earthly domain, but rather He was appointed to function as a high priest in a new sanctuary. And the appointment as High Priest, according to Psalm 110:4, follows the enthronement of Christ at His Father's right hand."[119]

The expression 'the Majesty' is found in only one other place in the Bible, back in chapter 1 verse 3:

---

[118] Griffith Thomas, *Go On*, p. 100.
[119] Pentecost, Dwight, quoted by Constable, Thomas L. *Expository Notes on Hebrews*, kindle 2023 edition.

"Who being the brightness of his glory, and the express image of his person, and upholding all things by the word of his power, when he had by himself purged our sins, sat down on the right hand of the Majesty on high;"

This verse is also a reference to His high priestly work. It is a technical point, but the purging of our sins was not part of that work in particular. It occurred at a moment in time where Christ fulfilled His part as the Sacrifice. This is said with reference to the types. In the Old Testament it was the priest who offered the sacrifice; the priest himself did not suffer and die. It was the sacrifice who did die, and with whom the priest identified when he placed his hand upon its head.

Now a related theological point—The sacrifices made atonement, or 'covered' sins, but could not 'take them away' (10:4, 10:11). They were killed, but God never 'poured out His wrath' on them. This is how justice is met, how God's holiness is satisfied. God must judge sin and the punishment is that wrath. Christ, as our propitiation (I John 4:10), took God's wrath on the cross. You may identify yourself with the Son (like the high priest did with the sacrifice on the Day of Atonement) and be saved from wrath, or you can have the wrath of God fall upon you for your sin. This is the only way it can be forgiven.[120]

---

[120] This point has been made already but wants an addition. Sin offends an infinite God, which makes it an infinite offense, and therefore His wrath must be infinitely

> *"Whom God hath set forth to be a propitiation through faith in his blood, to declare his righteousness for the remission of sins that are past, through the forbearance of God;"* Romans 3:25

Christ's current ministry as High Priest, with the sacrifice behind Him, is to bring us into the most holy place within the veil, with comfort and assurance. This is why we never read of Melchizedek offering any sacrifice. It's not that he never did, but that he is typical of Christ's current ministry (see footnote 109). This is what the author of Hebrews wants to deal with now that the personhood of the High Priest has been enumerated.

These mention of the "true tabernacle" is another proof of Christ's superiority, as He serves in a better sanctuary that the priests of old did.[121]

> *"For if he were on earth, he should not be a priest, seeing that there are priests that offer gifts according to the law:"* v. 4

This verse, in short order, affirms the diametric opposition of Christ's final priesthood to

---

satisfied. This is why Jesus, Who is eternal and Whose blood has infinite value, was the only One Who could ever satisfy that need. It is also why Hell must be eternal.

[121] Lane, *Hebrews*, p.116. It has been said by some that the 'true tabernacle' is Christ's body, now in heaven. This does not seem to make sense in the context, and we know that later, the book of Hebrews says the earthly tabernacle was a shadow of the heavenly.

that which mediated the law. The two *cannot* exist simultaneously.[122]

> *"Who serve unto the example and shadow of heavenly things, as Moses was admonished of God when he was about to make the tabernacle: for, See, saith he, that thou make all things according to the pattern shewed to thee in the mount."* v. 5

This verse states plainly that the earthly tabernacle was designed after the heavenly one. God gave Moses a vision while he was on the mountain (Was it simply of the tabernacle's construction, or did God show him the heavenly? It appears a window to heaven may have been opened, and even the people caught a glimpse of God's throne in 24:11-12). The verse quotes Exodus 25, and the 'mount' is Sinai, where the Ten Commandments were given. We will have more to say about the heavenly, or 'true' tabernacle in time.

> *"But now hath he obtained a more excellent ministry, by how much also he is the mediator of a better covenant, which was established upon better promises."* v. 6

---

[122] This is yet another reason why the dispensation of the Law cannot be reinstituted during the Tribulation Period as some say. Either Christ is the great High Priest or He isn't. Either His priestly service is earthly or it is heavenly. Either He mediates the law, or He doesn't. Either His ministry is final, or it's not. The book of Hebrews testifies unequivocally that He is High Priest, His service is heavenly, He does not mediate the law and His ministry is final.

Here is the introduction of a major aspect of the 'more excellent ministry' spoken of under verse 3. We also have the first mention of the 'better covenant.' This is the New Covenant that God has unconditionally promised for Israel. It will be described in detail later. Please keep in mind the main line of argument for the moment is Christ's superiority in His current work.

"For if that first covenant had been faultless, then should no place have been sought for the second. For finding fault with them, he saith, Behold, the days come, saith the Lord, when I will make a new covenant with the house of Israel and with the house of Judah: Not according to the covenant that I made with their fathers in the day when I took them by the hand to lead them out of the land of Egypt; because they continued not in my covenant, and I regarded them not, saith the Lord. For this is the covenant that I will make with the house of Israel after those days, saith the Lord; I will put my laws into their mind, and write them in their hearts: and I will be to them a God, and they shall be to me a people: And they shall not teach every man his neighbour, and every man his brother, saying, Know the Lord: for all shall know me, from the least to the greatest. For I will be merciful to their unrighteousness, and their sins and their iniquities will I remember no more. In that he saith, A new covenant, he hath made the first old. Now

that which decayeth and waxeth old is ready to vanish away." vv. 8-12

The first covenant was conditional, meaning that God said "If ye will..." This occurred in Exodus 19:5:

"Now therefore, if ye will obey my voice indeed, and keep my covenant, then ye shall be a peculiar treasure unto me above all people: for all the earth is mine:"

The children of Israel answered in verse 8:

"And all the people answered together, and said, All that the LORD hath spoken we will do. And Moses returned the words of the people unto the LORD."

This episode has often rightly been referred to as the 'marriage vows of Jehovah and Israel.' This is an apt comparison as marriage is also a holy covenant. The Old Covenant failed, not because God was not faithful, but because Israel did not live up to her end of the deal. God's faithfulness is untouched in the imperfect Old Covenant but is vindicated and exulted by the New Covenant. There are several points that should be observed when considering the transition from the Old Covenant to the New:

(1) <u>As with the Old Covenant, the New Covenant is made with a specific people-the Jewish people</u> (verse 10).

(2) <u>The New Covenant is not in effect yet</u>. This is proven by the expressions "after those days" and "is ready to vanish away." God has promised (like

in Exodus 19), but Israel has not accepted. This will happen at the end of the Tribulation. This event is described in several places in Scripture. Israel will be surrounded at that time, and in danger of complete annihilation at the hand of the armies of the earth.

> *"For I will gather all nations against Jerusalem to battle; and the city shall be taken, and the houses rifled, and the women ravished; and half of the city shall go forth into captivity, and the residue of the people shall not be cut off from the city."* Zechariah 14:2

> *"And shall go out to deceive the nations which are in the four quarters of the earth, Gog and Magog, to gather them together to battle: the number of whom is as the sand of the sea."* Revelation 20:8

Israel will then cry out to God for deliverance. This cry rings out through the Psalms and is typified by Peter when he is walking on the sea, surrounded by the tempest. At that moment a great hand will reach down:

> *"And I will pour upon the house of David, and upon the inhabitants of Jerusalem, the spirit of grace and of supplications: and they shall look upon me whom they have pierced, and they shall mourn for him, as one mourneth for his only son, and shall be in bitterness for him, as one that is in bitterness for his firstborn. In that day shall there be a great mourning in*

Jerusalem, as the mourning of Hadadrimmon in the valley of Megiddon."
Zechariah 12:10-11

But the mourning (Israel's repentance) does not last:

"Alas! for that day is great, so that none is like it: it is even the time of Jacob's trouble; but he shall be saved out of it."
Jeremiah 30:7

"And so all Israel shall be saved: as it is written, There shall come out of Sion the Deliverer, and shall turn away ungodliness from Jacob: For this is my covenant unto them, when I shall take away their sins."
Romans 11:26-27

Although the New Covenant is briefly described in our passage, the best place to go and read about it is in Jeremiah 30-33, which is what is partially quoted here.

(3) <u>The New Covenant is literal</u>. It is not a spiritual ideal.[123] This must be said because replacement theologians, wanting to claim the promises due to Israel, spiritualize the passage in Jeremiah. That passage, however, deals with real people and real promises (see point #1). The real

---

[123] It is a testament to faith that men such as Darby, Ironside, and MackIntosh, etc. held to a literal fulfillment of the New Covenant for Israel at a time when there was no Israel to speak of. If Replacement Theology could be forgiven before 1948, it certainly cannot now be.

people are promised a real piece of land.[124] Can anyone honestly say the items listed in verses 10-12 describe today's church? I trow not (Luke 17:9)!

> "Once we are permitted to make such plain words as 'Israel' and 'Judah' mean something else, there is no end to how we might interpret the Bible!"[125]

There is a covenant that we as the church will enter into. It is found in Hebrews 13:20.[126]

(4) <u>The imperfectness of the Old Covenant was anticipated</u>, not incidental. God knew Israel could not and would not abide by the Old Covenant. So why not just skip directly to the New Covenant? Why not spare the trouble, the death, the time? The answer is that man's fallenness and God's faithfulness is on grand display, the solution to sin is anticipated, and Jesus Christ gets all glory.

The superiority of the ministry of Christ is illustrated in the parable of the Good Samaritan.[127] This is found in Luke 10:30-35:

> *"And Jesus answering said, A certain*
> *man went down from Jerusalem to Jericho,*
> *and fell among thieves, which stripped him*

---

[124] See the great work *The Millennial Kingdom* by Walvoord, John F. (Zondervan 1959).

[125] Wiersbe, Warren W, *The Bible Exposition Commentary-volume 2* (Victor Books, 1989), p. 306.

[126] Newell, *Hebrews*, p. 258.

[127] This is not to say that it is the primary point, but that there are parallels.

of his raiment, and wounded him, and departed, leaving him half dead. And by chance there came down a certain priest that way: and when he saw him, he passed by on the other side. And likewise a Levite, when he was at the place, came and looked on him, and passed by on the other side. But a certain Samaritan, as he journeyed, came where he was: and when he saw him, he had compassion on him, And went to him, and bound up his wounds, pouring in oil and wine, and set him on his own beast, and brought him to an inn, and took care of him. And on the morrow when he departed, he took out two pence, and gave them to the host, and said unto him, Take care of him; and whatsoever thou spendest more, when I come again, I will repay thee."

You will notice that the first man to come along was a priest. The second was a Levite. Neither of these men were of help to the beleaguered man. There are many reasons why this could be. It has been said that the priest was ritually clean, and that he could not help the man without defiling and excluding himself from temple service. The Levite was perhaps worried about the legal ramifications or expense of involving himself with this poor man. If this be true, religion got in the way of helping him. The law would not be ignored. Yet one came along who, being half Jewish (probably on his mother's side) was willing to lower himself and help the man, whatever be the cost. The priesthood came and went, the law came and went. Someone new came along at last, and the man was restored to life. Can you see Jesus Christ in this?

(5). <u>The New Covenant is Unconditional</u>.

"How great a contrast between the old and the new covenant! In the one God demands of sinful man: 'Thou shalt.' In the other, God promises: 'I will.'"[128]

---

[128] Saphir, Adolph *The Epistle to the Hebrews-volume 2* (Loizeaux Brothers, 1946), p. 413.

HEBREWS CHAPTER 9

"Because of the fact that mathematical truths are necessary truths, no actual 'information', in the technical sense, passes to the discoverer. All the information was there all the time. It was just a matter of putting things together and 'seeing' the answer!" – Sir Roger Penrose[129]

"Then verily the first covenant had also ordinances of divine service, and a worldly sanctuary. For there was a tabernacle made; the first, wherein was the candlestick, and the table, and the shewbread; which is called the sanctuary. And after the second veil, the tabernacle which is called the Holiest of all;" Hebrews 9:1-3

Once again, we must not let the chapter division break the train of reasoning. We are moving from the *service* of the great High Priest to the *sanctuary* of the great High Priest. The author of Hebrews does this by comparing the earthly tabernacle to the heavenly.[130]

---

[129] Penrose, Roger *The Emperor's New Mind* (Oxford University Press, 1989), p. 428.

[130] A point must be made about the use of the word 'covenant' here. Replacement theology would say that these verses prove that we are indeed operating under the New Covenant, because the author is comparing Israel's tabernacle to the one Christ ministers in for the church today. That this is not the point that is being made is proven by (1) the heavenly tabernacle existed prior to the earthly, as stated

The furniture of the tabernacle, as the tabernacle itself, speaks of Christ. If an interpretation about the typology of an individual element does not say something of Christ, it cannot be accepted. For instance, if you read that the twelve loaves (shewbread) stand for the twelve disciples, you should disregard it. If you hear that the four rings on the ark represent the four Gospels, put it out with the trash. This writer has heard that the candlestick is the Holy Spirit that illumines the Word, and that the shewbread is the Word of God (two rows of 6 = 66 books). We must respectfully disagree. Jesus Christ is the "light of the world" (John 8:12), and the "bread from heaven" (John 6:32, 33, 50, 51, 58).[131]

The Bible never calls the 'most Holy Place' the 'Holy of Holies.' It is called here 'the Holiest of all.'

---

in the last chapter, (2) the tabernacle was a type of Christ walking the earth in the midst of His people, which He will do again, but not until the Millennium, (3) verse 11 speaks of 'good things to come' as well as ministering presently, (4) the text shifts from speaking of the covenants to the 'new testament' (the institution, not the last third of the Bible).

[131] We do not deny that there is a relationship between the shewbread and the Word of God. The shewbread was to remain before God continually. The Word of God liveth and abideth forever (I Peter 1:23) and is forever settled in heaven (Psalm 119:89), but it must be admitted that the 'Word' of John 1:1 has a close relationship to this word, and both are the revelation of the Person of Christ. Christ fulfilled the type of the shewbread, and it is no longer needed. God's Word is still in use. The Bible is careful to tell us that the candlestick was of 'beaten work.' The Holy Spirit was never beaten, but our Lord certainly was.

The careful reader will notice that two 'veils' are mentioned in these verses. The second veil was embroidered with cherubim which 'guarded the way into the Holiest of all.' Remember that Adam and Eve were driven from the presence of the Lord after the Fall, and,

> *"he placed at the east of the garden of Eden Cherubims, and a flaming sword which turned every way, to keep the way of the tree of life."* Genesis 3:24b

The cherubim were placed there for Adam and Eve's protection, just as the barrier and cherubim were for the priests.

> *"Which had the golden censer, and the ark of the covenant overlaid round about with gold, wherein was the golden pot that had manna, and Aaron's rod that budded, and the tables of the covenant;"* v. 4

Because of the Greek word behind 'censer' (θυμιαστήριον, or thumiesterion), and because of the lack of a mention of a censer in the construction of the tabernacle in Exodus, some commentators have chosen to designate the altar of incense in this verse. If they had only looked a little farther, they may have noticed this passage:

> *"And Aaron shall bring the bullock of the sin offering, which is for himself, and shall make an atonement for himself, and for his house, and shall kill the bullock of the sin offering which is for himself: And he shall take a censer full of burning coals of fire from*

> *off the altar before the LORD, and his hands
> full of sweet incense beaten small, and bring
> it within the vail: And he shall put the incense
> upon the fire before the LORD, that the cloud
> of the incense may cover the mercy seat that
> is upon the testimony, that he die not:"*
> Leviticus 16:11-13

This passage is especially relevant because this occurred on the day of atonement. This incense is closely connected with prayer. Notice Revelation 8:3-4:

> *"And another angel came and stood
> at the altar, having a golden censer; and
> there was given unto him much incense, that
> he should offer it with the prayers of all saints
> upon the golden altar which was before the
> throne. And the smoke of the incense, which
> came with the prayers of the saints,
> ascended up before God out of the angel's
> hand."*

This writer has heard and read that the incense *is* the prayers of the saints, however, careful reading shows that the incense goes *with* the prayers. If the elements of the tabernacle are pictures of Christ, then the incense, being an element of tabernacle worship, is in some way typical of Christ as well. The high priest sends the incense before him into the most Holy Place (God's presence, His throne), then enters himself, on behalf of the people, "that he die not:". If our formula for typology holds true, Christ goes, with our prayers, into the presence of God, and intercedes on our behalf. The incense may then be typical of His operation through the Spirit, which makes, not only His service, but our prayers well-pleasing to God (Romans 8:26).

Every Christian has the commission of intercessory prayer (I Timothy 2:1). We are to go before God in prayer on behalf of others. To not do so is to be derelict in our duty.

One final thought on this subject of prayer and the high priest—if you will remember, the comments under 5:9 were to the effect that the 'perfecting' of Christ in that passage was about fitting Him to be the High Priest on our behalf. Part of that process included prayer as seen in 5:7. Some things the high priest of the old covenant did on that great Day of Atonement (Yom Kippur) was offer a sin offering for himself, and the people. He also had a ritual cleansing. These things Christ did not need, as He was sinless (see chapter 5 again). However, once this was done, the priest put on a linen garment, put in the incense, then offered the blood on the mercy seat. The linen garment is 'the days of his flesh' and the incense was the 'prayers and supplications' both found in Hebrews 5:7.

Some have complained about the fact that the verse seems to say that the pot of manna, Aaron's rod, and the tables of the covenant (Ten Commandments) were *inside* the ark, whereas the Old Testament says they were placed *by* the ark (Exodus 16:33 and Numbers 17:10). Again, a later reference would have cleared this up. Check out II Chronicles 5:10:

> *"There was nothing in the ark save the two tables which Moses put therein at Horeb, when the LORD made a covenant with the children of Israel, when they came out of Egypt."*[132]

It seems clear that when the tabernacle was transported, these items were placed inside the ark and carried that way until the building of the Solomonic temple.

> *"And over it the cherubims of glory shadowing the mercyseat; of which we cannot now speak particularly."* v. 5

The author seems to want to go into further detail about the mercy seat atop the ark, but refrains. It is reminiscent of the statement in 5:11 concerning Melchizedek.

> *"Now when these things were thus ordained, the priests went always into the first tabernacle, accomplishing the service of God. But into the second went the high priest alone once every year, not without blood, which he offered for himself, and for the errors of the people:"* vv. 6,7

---

[132] The law remained even after the ark came to rest. This is symbolic of at least two things: (1) Only Christ was able to keep the law, (2) Christ fulfilled all things, but that does not mean the law is done away with "Think not that I am come to destroy the law, or the prophets: I am not come to destroy, but to fulfil." Mark 5:17. Also, (3) the law is deadly to a sinful people (I Corinthians 15:56), but here it lies, inside this chest, covered with blood. "There need be no dread..." - Meyer.

This has been covered already, but bears repeating at this point. We are illustrating the 'weakness' of the old. The priests entered through the first veil continually, but the high priest alone went in through the second veil once a year. While 'once a year' is placed next to 'daily' as a type of Christ's one-time entry, the fact remains that the shadow was indeed repeated year by year.

> *"The Holy Ghost this signifying, that the way into the holiest of all was not yet made manifest, while as the first tabernacle was yet standing: Which was a figure for the time then present, in which were offered both gifts and sacrifices, that could not make him that did the service perfect, as pertaining to the conscience; Which stood only in meats and drinks, and divers washings, and carnal ordinances, imposed on them until the time of reformation."* vv. 8-10

The first thing to notice about this verse is the continuation of referring to the Old Testament scriptures as the voice of the Holy Ghost. The author of Hebrews makes no qualms about Biblical inspiration or inerrancy.

The physical tabernacle, with its veils and requirements for entry illustrated in a tangible way that the way into the Holiest was closed to the people. The verse is also saying that the gifts and sacrifices were more figures (or shadows).[133] We

---

[133] The underlying Greek is παραβολὴ, a word used elsewhere for 'parable.' This does not affect our understanding; we state it for interest only.

cannot give them more stress or power than God does. We cannot say they had salvific power when the Bible doesn't say they did. The sacrifices were types only.

Not only did the rites not save in the sense of escape from condemnation, but verse 9 says they were unable to cleanse the conscience. Imagine looking into the eyes of the innocent animal that was about to be killed on account of sins you have committed. Would this relieve your conscience? It may add to it, especially if you are an animal lover!

The word translated "washings" in Greek is βαπτισμός (baptismos). This leads those who make use of sprinkling as a means of baptism to claim that all the 'washings' of the Old Testament were sprinklings, therefore there is no basis for immersion as the only means of baptism for the New Testament church. This is blatantly false. The washings of the Old Testament are ritual cleansings wherein the priests bathed their entire bodies (Exodus 30:20). Some sacrifices were washed, and every vessel used in the tabernacle was washed. Sprinkling would not accomplish this. Furthermore, the word used in our text *cannot* be made into a sprinkling. The word never means 'sprinkling.' *Only* 'immersion.'[134] Even furthermore, the Christian baptism does not have its type in the Old Testament sprinklings *or* the ritual cleansings. It is a picture of Christ's burial. Not even the spiritual

---

[134] Kittel, Gerhard, ed. *Theological Dictionary of the New Testament (TDNT)* (Eerdman's Publishing Company, 1964), p. 545.

'baptism into Christ' has its type in the washings or sprinklings.

> *"But Christ being come an high priest of good things to come, by a greater and more perfect tabernacle, not made with hands, that is to say, not of this building; Neither by the blood of goats and calves, but by his own blood he entered in once into the holy place, having obtained eternal redemption for us." vv. 11,12*

Here is the transition from picture to reality, from the depiction to what was being depicted, from the earthly rudiment to the spiritual actuality.

Verse 12 is heralded by some Hyper-Calvinists as the greatest refutation of unlimited atonement in the entirety of the Bible. This is because the verse says that Christ's entering obtained eternal redemption for us. This redemption, they say, cannot be *potential* redemption, but *actual* because it guarantees its own end. If the redemption spoken of here was universal, all would be saved. If it is only potential, it is ineffective for some, and therefore God does not grant what Jesus has paid for. Christ's entering, then, obtains redemption for the elect only.[135] This they justify by the prepositional phrase "for us." What is the problem with this? There are several. First, (1) the 'entering in' of Christ is in His capacity as High Priest. It should be clear by now that our salvation is not a function of Christ's High

---

[135] See almost any Reformed work on the subject from Owen on.

Priesthood, but rather a result of His substitutionary sacrifice. (2) Typologically, the sacrifice on the Day of Atonement, performed by the high priest, was on behalf of people *who were already saved*.[136] (3) Although 'redemption' goes hand-in-hand with justification, it is not one and the same. We have a future redemption (Romans 8:23, Ephesians 1:14,), and a present redemption, having to do with the breaking of the power of sin in our lives.

> "A ransom is the securing of a release by the payment of a price. To be redeemed is to be delivered by the payment of a ransom. Redemption presupposes some kind of bondage or captivity."[137]

This is the redemption we are dealing with. The blood of Jesus broke forever the power of sin in our lives. We do not have to bear up under sin but can live in victory and serve with confidence.

Even proponents of limited atonement are careful to separate justification and redemption.[138] The proof that this verse is referring to the latter definition (current redemption) comes in the very next two verses:

---

[136] Anderson, *Types*, p. 50.

[137] Vance, Laurence M. *The Other Side of Calvinism* (Vance Publications, Revised Edition, 2014), p. 417.

[138] See https://heidelbergseminary.org/2019/10/the-doctrine-of-limited-atonement-8-scriptural-proofs/ *"The death of Christ actually justifies* the believer because His shed blood was the propitiation for sin and was acceptable to God. Redemption is the actual setting free from the bondage of sin by the blood of Christ to serve the living God."

"For if the blood of bulls and of goats, and the ashes of an heifer sprinkling the unclean, sanctifieth to the purifying of the flesh: How much more shall the blood of Christ, who through the eternal Spirit offered himself without spot to God, purge your conscience from dead works to serve the living God?" vv. 13,14

This is type and antetype in action. There is a one-to-one correspondence. The blood of bulls and goats, and the red heifer sprinkling were for people who were already redeemed from Egypt. Notice that the verse does not say "the blood of a lamb." The Passover lamb not only shed its blood, but it was partaken of, and its blood was applied to individual houses on behalf of individual persons. Christ's High Priesthood facilitates holiness and communion with God, but the application of blood to the dwelling (earthly body II Corinthians 5:1 etc.) is what purchased the initial redemption typified by the Passover. This initial individual application of the blood of the lamb/Lamb is a prerequisite to all the benefits of God's people, regardless of dispensation or covenant.

A simplified version of everything above would run as follows: The Old Testament type of salvation is a combination of the Passover through the crossing of the Red Sea. Everything that follows that has to do with God's relationship with those who had come in under the Passover. The Levitical priesthood occurs *after* the Passover, and so has everything to do with Israel's relationship with God, and nothing to do with salvation. Just the same,

Christ's High Priesthood occurs after our salvation, and has everything to do with our relationship with God, and nothing to do with salvation, other than that it is prerequisite.

Can you see the glorious accuracy of the Bible with its types? Surely, had a man written it, he would have missed the mark somewhere along the line in constructing such a complex system of types and pictures, especially ≈1450 years removed from the antetype!

Before these verses are put behind us, the idea of Christ entering the Holy Place by His blood must be addressed. The dominating view in theological circles today is that the blood of Christ (the shedding) stands only for death—that there is no intrinsic value in the blood itself. Here is a quote by one of the leading proponents of this view:

> ". . .there's no sense in getting teary-eyed and mystical about blood. And we sing hymns, "There's power in the blood," et cetera, and we don't want to get preoccupied with blood. The only importance the blood of Jesus has is that it showed He died. There is no saving in that blood itself. We cannot say that the very blood of Jesus, His physical blood, is what atones for sin; it is His death that atones for sin, His bloodshed was an act of death. And so, we do not want to become preoccupied with fantasizing about some mystical blood that's floating around somewhere. It is by His sacrificial offering of Himself. It is by His death that we are

redeemed. Bloodshed is only the picture of His death."[139]

They further go on to say that Christ did not physically offer His actual blood to God in the heavenly tabernacle, on the heavenly mercy seat. If this is true, and that it is only Christ's death that matters for us, let's ask a few questions:

(1) If the blood of Christ does not get placed on a heavenly mercy seat, why did God require the Old Testament priest to do this? Could he not have killed the sin offering and left it lying in situ?

(2) If the blood itself is not important, why, in the Last Supper, does Jesus include unfermented wine in the ceremony? Why did Melchizedek? Why do we?

(3) Why did God have the Israelites place the blood on the sides and lintel of their door during Passover? Why not hang a sign?

(4) Why is our Bible so pervaded by blood? It is found in nearly 450 places! It sounds like God may have been a little "preoccupied by the blood!"

(5) If Jesus is still a physical man (John 20:27), why is it strange that His blood might be physically offered?[140]

---

[139] MacArthur, John, Grace To You website, https://www.gty.org/library/sermons-library/80-44/the-blood-of-christ, accessed 8/26/23.

[140] Men such as J. Vernon McGee and Lewis Sperry Chafer agree with this view.

Though it is impossible to describe, the teaching seems clear. God is not haphazard in His typology. The blood is not only important, but preeminent. The Israelites could not stop with the killing of the Passover lamb. When the angel of death went through Goshen, the death of the Passover Lamb would not have availed *had the blood not been applied*. Further, no one could partake of the Passover without passing through that blood! Just the same, the death of the sin offering would have done nothing had the priest not taken its blood into the most Holy Place, and Christ's work would not have been complete had He not offered the blood to God on our behalf.

"For the death of the sacrifice was only a means towards an end, that end being the shedding and sprinkling of the blood, by which the atonement was really made"[141]

"There are many people who believe in the shedding of the blood; they believe that the Lord Jesus died, but they have not appropriated His work for themselves, and so are not resting under the sprinkled blood. To have rested only on the fact that the lamb had been killed would not have brought safety; but having done what God told them, the children of Israel were safe."[142]

---

[141] Edersheim, Alfred, *The Temple-It's Ministry & Services* (Religious Tract Society), p. 115.

[142] Habershon, Ada R. *A Study of the Types*, (Kregel Publications, 1973). p. 37.

"And for this cause he is the mediator of the new testament, that by means of death, for the redemption of the transgressions that were under the first testament, they which are called might receive the promise of eternal inheritance. For where a testament is, there must also of necessity be the death of the testator. For a testament is of force after men are dead: otherwise it is of no strength at all while the testator liveth. Whereupon neither the first testament was dedicated without blood." vv. 15-18

"...for this cause..." For what cause? It is the virtue and efficacy of His sacrificial offering and priestly service from verse 14. He now mediates between holy God and sinful man under the auspices of the 'new testament.'

Every English translation since the Authorized Version of 1611 has changed 'testament' to 'covenant' in these verses. There are two reasons for this: (1) the underlying Greek word is the same. (2) There is theological bias.

The Greek work διαθήκη (diatheke) is one of a couple of words that can be translated 'covenant.' It is context that determines which word is to be used. The context of our passage is not difficult to determine, as it is spelled out plainly in verses 16 and 17. For it to be a 'testament', the death of the testator must be present.[143] Here is a brief survey to establish the point:

Genesis 6:18 and in chapter 9 we have the Noahic Covenant. No death of a testator.

Genesis 12 begins the description of the Abrahamic Covenant. No death.[144]

Genesis 21:27: A covenant is made between Abraham and Abimelech. No death.

Genesis 26:28: Isaac makes a covenant with Abimelech. No death.

Exodus 19:5 is the start of the Mosaic Covenant. No death.

Numbers 25:12: God makes a covenant with Eleazar. No death.

Joshua 24:25: No death.

I Samuel 11:1: No death.

I Samuel 18:3: No death.

I Kings 20:34: No death.

II Kings 11:17: No death.

---

[143] Wuest gets it right (*Hebrews,* p. 162-163). Griffith Thomas, Darby, and Grant get it partially right (see *Let Us Go On*, p. 116-117).

[144] Some have argued that the ritual performed in Chapter 15 where the covenant is expanded is the death required. This is highly debatable. The Abrahamic Covenant is revisited many times with no reference to death; also, according to our author, we are discussing testaments, of which the first is clearly said to be that of Exodus 24 (see vv. 19-21).

See also II Kings 23:3, I Chronicles 11:3, II Chronicles 7:18, Ezra 10:3, Nehemiah 9:38, Job 31:1, Jeremiah 31:33, Daniel 9:27, Matthew 26:15, etc.

What we observe is that a 'covenant' occurs between two living persons, and a 'testament' is made between one who dies and benefits the one who lives.

There are other reasons to retain the A.V. reading in this passage. Rendering it 'covenant' would be a striking redundancy after the description of the New Covenant in chapter 8:6-13.[145] Making only 16 and 17 refer to a testament and the rest a covenant[146] gives a very disjointed reading. Also, what is being discussed in this chapter has everything to do with Christ's death, and the shedding of His blood, not the New Covenant specifically.

Romans 6 is the best commentary available describing what the death of Christ has done for us versus His resurrected life. His death is the basis for our forgiveness, but it is also the breaking of the power of sin in our lives. The central verse of Romans 6 is verse 6:

---

[145]Anderson in *Types*, has a note on page 56 that reads in part "...in his *Light from the Ancient East* Prof. Deissmann shows that with all Greek-speaking peoples in the first century, the only meaning in common use was "testament."

[146] This is what is meant by 'partially right' in the footnote above. Hobbs, who claims to know what the author of Hebrews was thinking (p. 91), does the same. Oh, to have these powers!

> *"Knowing this, that our old man is crucified with him, that the body of sin might be destroyed, that henceforth we should not serve sin."*

There are other places where the word 'testament' is found. The so-called 'Last Supper' was the establishment by Christ of the ordinance of communion. Make of it what you will, but Christ refers to the cup only as being 'of the new testament.' The bread represented His body, which was broken, but His death came afterward. This seems to place greater emphasis on the blood.

Finally, II Corinthians 3:6 says:

> *"Who also hath made us able ministers of the new testament; not of the letter, but of the spirit: for the letter killeth, but the spirit giveth life."*

The "us" of this verse is the church, to whom Paul writes. These are blood-bought saints who have the ministry of reconciling sinners to God by the propagation of the Gospel of Christ. The second half of the verse is out of our present subject but dispenses with the idea that the giving of the Catholic Mass is the ministration of the New Testament, for it is of the life-giving spirit. Indeed, our communion, or Lord's Supper is only a memorial of its establishment.

The 'old testament' to which verse 18 refers is that which gives the Old Testament of our Bible its name. Genesis and part of Exodus give the history leading up to the Old Testament, while the rest of the Old Testament books give the history of the testament itself. The giving of this first testament is found in Exodus 24, which our author will now relate.

"For when Moses had spoken every precept to all the people according to the law, he took the blood of calves and of goats, with water, and scarlet wool, and hyssop, and sprinkled both the book, and all the people, Saying, This is the blood of the testament which God hath enjoined unto you. Moreover he sprinkled with blood both the tabernacle, and all the vessels of the ministry." vv. 19-21

What the author is getting at is a comparison between the blood of the Old Testament, that of calves and goats, and the superior blood of our Lord Jesus Christ, the Lamb of God. It is interesting that the book of the Law was sprinkled as well. Over the last two thousand years, there have been countless stories of men and women who held to God's Book at the cost of blood. It cost men of great fame like William Tyndale his life. It also cost thousands of nameless people throughout history their lives, though we may never hear their stories. It costs people their lives today in places like China, North Korea, Nigeria, and across the Middle East. These are precious and sobering thoughts, but the most significant cost of blood was the that of the Lord Jesus Christ.

The Old Testament was 'in force' by the death of the calves and goats. These stood for the blood of Christ that would one day be shed. When it finally was, the New Testament was (and now is) in force. We would be familiar with the phrase 'last will and testament,' and associate it with instructions as to how that will should be carried out.

A good way to think about the difference between the testaments and covenants for us today is to limit the term 'testament' to only those things that Jesus did through His death, and 'covenant' to those things that God promises based upon Who He is.

> "We need Him who 'became dead' for pardon and cleansing; we need Him who is 'alive for evermore' for present participation in His life and present sitting with Him in heavenly places, and for the ultimate eternal entrance there, whence we shall go no more out."[147]

> *"And almost all things are by the law purged with blood; and without shedding of blood is no remission."* v. 22

This verse should have been the death of the idea that blood merely stands for death. Regardless of how you think the event of verse 15 went down, it should be clear that blood is required. The blood is applied to everything: the altar, the mercy seat, the implements of service, the book, the people, and on and on. If death alone was the requirement, why doesn't this verse say that? Why is blood

---

[147] Maclaren, *Expositions*, p. 75.

specifically mentioned so many times? Why would God make such a big deal out of it?

> *"For the life of the flesh is in the blood: and I have given it to you upon the altar to make an atonement for your souls: for it is the blood that maketh an atonement for the soul."* Leviticus 17:11

The verse says that the *blood* is what makes the atonement, not the *death*.

Jesus' blood was no mere man's blood. It was special. Not only was it not corrupt, but it was God's blood! If you think God does not have blood, take a quick look at Acts 20:28:

> *"Take heed therefore unto yourselves, and to all the flock, over the which the Holy Ghost hath made you overseers, to feed the church of God, which he hath purchased with his own blood."*

The fact that the blood covered everything in sight should remind the reader of Colossians 1:20:

> *"And, having made peace through the blood of his cross, by him to reconcile all things unto himself; by him, I say, whether they be things in earth, or things in heaven."*

Not only was blood required to be applied to the heavenly mercy seat, but it has further applications for the believer.

(1) <u>The blood is applied to the believer at salvation.</u> This may be the key to why certain theologians reject the efficacy of the blood. This application

happens *in time*. This is important because we are not saved until that point. We do not become 'the elect' until then. By making the death the important thing, you can push it back to 'before the foundation of the world.' This is not to say God doesn't know who will be saved, but that our willful decision in time is the nexus between Christ's work and its application to us.

(2) <u>The blood continues to be applied for the purpose of sanctification in the believer's life.</u> This was the purpose for the entire system of Old Testament law![148] Every sacrifice pictured the same blood, but every sacrifice had a different purpose. For the Christian in the Age of Grace, the same blood is for justification *and* sanctification! Two verses that say definitively that the blood applies to sanctification are:

> *"But now in Christ Jesus ye who sometimes were far off are made nigh by the blood of Christ."* Ephesians 2:13

And:

> *"Elect according to the foreknowledge of God the Father, through sanctification of the Spirit, unto obedience and sprinkling of the blood of Jesus Christ: Grace unto you, and peace, be multiplied."* I Peter 1:2

We say, along with Brother Meyer, "Why should we be ashamed of the blood of Christ?"

---

[148] Again, we would stress that the Passover is the sacrifice that most closely typifies salvation. No one was given the law that had not been redeemed by the Passover.

Commenting on I John 5:6, he goes on further to say:

> "Had it been water only, we had been undone. Water might do for respectable sinners-fifty-pence debtors, Pharisees, who are not sinners as other men. But some of us feel water would be of no avail at all. Our sins are so deep-dyed, so inveterate, so fast, that nothing but blood could set us free. Blood must atone for us. Blood must buy us. Blood must cleanse us."[149]

> *"It was therefore necessary that the patterns of things in the heavens should be purified with these; but the heavenly things themselves with better sacrifices than these. For Christ is not entered into the holy places made with hands, which are the figures of the true; but into heaven itself, now to appear in the presence of God for us: Nor yet that he should offer himself often, as the high priest entereth into the holy place every year with blood of others; For then must he often have suffered since the foundation of the world: but now once in the end of the world hath he appeared to put away sin by the sacrifice of himself. And as it is appointed unto men once to die, but after this the judgment: So Christ was once offered to bear the sins of many; and unto them that look for him shall he appear the second time without sin unto salvation."* vv. 23-28

---

[149] Meyer, *Holiest*, p. 118.

This is a beautiful description of Christ's work as both sacrifice and priest. Be careful in verse 23 to see that it was necessary to purify the 'patterns' with 'these' (the blood of calves/bulls and goats), and the heavenly with the better sacrifices. There are two reasons that the heavenly needed to be purified as well as the earthly, though the first is somewhat controversial:

(1) Satan sinned as described in Isaiah 14 and Ezekiel 28. That sin was before God in heaven, and therefore must be purged in that realm as well as ours.

(2) God's intention is to dwell with man. Whatever the heavenly mercy seat looks like or of what it consists, it is associated with His throne and man could never be in the presence of God without the covering of the blood (see Revelation 21:3).

> "Not without blood! In earth and heaven, in each moment of our life, in each thought and act of worship, this word reigns supreme. There can be no fellowship with God, but in the blood, in the death, of His blessed Son."[150]

The one death, the one entering of Christ stated here will be expounded in chapter 10. For the phrase "in the end of the world," see the comments under chapter 1, verse 2 of this commentary.

---

[150] Murray, Andrew *The Holiest of All* (Fleming H. Revell Company, New Jersey), p. 316.

HEBREWS CHAPTER 10

"There will come a time when you think everything is finished. That will be the beginning." – Tell Sackett[151]

"For the law having a shadow of good things to come, and not the very image of the things, can never with those sacrifices which they offered year by year continually make the comers thereunto perfect. For then would they not have ceased to be offered? because that the worshippers once purged should have had no more conscience of sins. But in those sacrifices there is a remembrance again made of sins every year. For it is not possible that the blood of bulls and of goats should take away sins." Hebrews 10:1-4

This chapter begins simply enough. Because the physical trappings of the law (the tabernacle and sacrifices, etc.), were only a shadow, they cannot effect God's desired end, the perfection of His saints. The term 'perfect' here is in the same sense as the previous instances (2:10, 5:9, 7:19, etc.), that is complete, or suited. The proof the author gives is the fact that they had to be repeated. Once again, we are reminded that the sacrifices and washings 'purged' only ceremonially but could not reach the innermost man. There was a continual reminder to God's people of the sins of

---

[151] L'amour, Louis *Lonely On the Mountain* (Random House Publishing Group, 1980), p. 1.

the past year, adding to the ones committed in the years before that.

> "The conscience of a devout Jew resembled the conscience of a devout Roman Catholic today. The Catholic must go to his 'priest,' to the 'confessional' telling this man-made priest sins; and the promise is, that the 'priest' resorts to the figment of the 'unbloody sacrifice' of 'the Mass,' for he knows not the finished work of Christ, by Whose blood sin was *put away* once for all, on the Cross. What a Romish priest finds and the Jew of old found, is **a remembrance of sins**."[152]

For the Jew, the Day of Atonement was a confession (Leviticus 16:21). Jesus, having fulfilled the whole Law, including the Day of Atonement, made 'confession' before men obsolete. We have but one Priest, and He is the only One to Whom we confess.

This is yet another importance of the application of the blood of Christ to the actual believer. We pray that our sins be purged by the blood, and it is efficacious. Only the shed blood of Christ is effective in removing the guilt associated with sin.

---

[152] Newell, *Hebrews*, p. 331. Newell recognizes that God established the Levitical system and limits his comparison. A closer comparison would be this Catholic system with the Jewish system still in existence when Hebrews was written, after Christ had risen, but Hebrews is comparing the two sacrifices God had respect to.

"To have no more consciousness of sins does not mean that true believers are henceforth blissfully unaware of sinfulness in their lives. The statement refers to the consciousness of sin's guilt as being still objectively unremoved."[153]

Verse 4 tells of the impossibility of the old sacrifices to take care of the problem of sin. God had respect to them when offered in faith, but they only pushed judgment for sin into the future, awaiting the perfect sacrifice, the one that *could* take away sin. If the Law had saving power, Christ would not have had to die, but only to have lived His perfect life. Conversely, Christ living His perfect life did not save anyone. It was an example to follow, and a qualifier to His sacrifice and priesthood, as well as proof of His deity.

The inability of the Law to *"take away sins"* is why the Old Testament saints did not go to heaven upon death. They went to a place commonly referred to as 'Abraham's bosom.' This idea is substantiated in Luke 16:22-23.

> *"And it came to pass, that the beggar died, and was carried by the angels into Abraham's bosom: the rich man also died, and was buried; And in hell he lift up his eyes, being in torments, and seeth Abraham afar off, and Lazarus in his bosom."*

---

[153] Kent, Homer A., Jr. *The Epistle to the Hebrews* (Baker Book House, 1983), p. 185.

As you can see, the rich man could see where Lazarus was, but he could not get there himself. In verse 26, the Bible says that a 'great gulf' was placed between them. If hell is real (and it is) then this place is also real. The only conclusion that can be drawn is that hell and the place known as Abraham's bosom are adjacent to one another. When Jesus died, He made the way to heaven open to these saints and went to lead them out. Ephesians 4:8, quoting Psalm 68:18, describes this when it says:

> *"Wherefore he saith, When he ascended up on high, he led captivity captive, and gave gifts unto men."*

It is said that Abraham's Bosom is the same as 'paradise' (Luke 23:43). There are issues with this: (1) paradise would have had to have been taken from the center of the earth, up to heaven. It is clear from Revelation 2:7 that paradise is currently in heaven. Also, the only other reference to paradise (II Corinthians 12:4) puts it in heaven. It is never called paradise while in the earth. (2) If the taking up to heaven idea is true, there is a timing problem. When did this happen? The thief on the cross is told that he would be with Jesus in paradise *that day*. Did he go *down* to paradise, awaiting Jesus' rescue? Jesus was *already dead* when the thief's legs were broken (John 19:32-33).[154] These things considered, it is certainly not

---

[154] There is also a huge problem for the so-called 'moderate dispensationalist.' If saints under the Law died and went to Abraham's bosom, and the Tribulation dispensation returns to being under the Law, where do those saints go?

impossible that they are the same, only slightly difficult. It remains this writer's opinion.

What is important to glean is that no matter who you are or when you lived, it is only through the blood of Christ that anyone enters heaven. This is stated so clearly in 9:15, it is a wonder that anyone ever missed it:

> *"for the redemption of the transgressions that were under the first testament, they which are called might receive the promise of eternal inheritance."*

There will be no one in heaven that can claim anything else for entrance- so says the book of Hebrews repeatedly. To do so would rob the Lord Jesus Christ of the glory due His name.

> *"Wherefore when he cometh into the world, he saith, Sacrifice and offering thou wouldest not, but a body hast thou prepared me: In burnt offerings and sacrifices for sin thou hast had no pleasure. Then said I, Lo, I come (in the volume of the book it is written of me,) to do thy will, O God. Above when he said, Sacrifice and offering and burnt offerings and offering for sin thou wouldest not, neither hadst pleasure therein; which are offered by the law; Then said he, Lo, I come to do thy will, O God. He taketh away*

They would not be allowed in heaven. This writer heard one of these preachers say that Abraham's bosom must return to earth for the Tribulation! Can you see what tangled messes one can get in trying to squeeze their pet doctrines into the Scripture?

the first, that he may establish the second. By the which will we are sanctified through the offering of the body of Jesus Christ once for all." vv. 5-10

The author of this marvelous book doubles down on the insufficiency of the Old Testament sacrifices. He goes so far as to refer to the fact that God had 'no pleasure' in them. He then quotes Psalm 40:6-8:

*"Sacrifice and offering thou didst not desire; **mine ears hast thou opened:** burnt offering and sin offering hast thou not required. Then said I, Lo, I come: in the volume of the book it is written of me, I delight to do thy will, O my God: yea, thy law is within my heart."*

You may notice a difference in the two passages. The differing phrase in Psalms (in bold) is a different view of the same thing. Here in Hebrews, we have a 'body' that was broken for us. In Psalms, we have ears that have been opened. What can the Holy Spirit be saying to us by adjusting this quote? It was following the breaking of His body that Christ entered into His high Priestly work, and it is as High Priest that Christ ministers to saints in this way:

"For the eyes of the Lord are over the righteous, and his ears are open unto their prayers:" I Peter 3:12

The connecting theme is obedience. Jesus had a will of His own, but His will never, even for a moment, departed from the will of His Father. To do so would have been sinful. He had all power, but He chose to operate ever under the power of the third Person of the Godhead, the Holy Ghost. He did not come to merely offer a sacrifice perfectly, as a High Priest, but to present His own body as the perfect Sacrifice. There is no real comparison between this and the Old Testament sacrifices. They are only hints, like the shadow a bottle casts versus the act of drinking the soda.

> *"But made himself of no reputation, and took upon him the form of a servant, and was made in the likeness of men: And being found in fashion as a man, he humbled himself, and became obedient unto death, even the death of the cross."* Philippians 2:7-8

Notice 'in the volume of the book it is written of me,'. The 'volume of the book' means its entirety. The way we know the books of the Bible belong in the canon is that they testify of Christ on each and every page.

The term 'sanctified' in verse ten mirrors the word 'perfect' in verse 1. We are not only concerned with salvation, but like most of the rest of this great book, Christian maturity as well. The clue to this is "the offering of the body of Jesus Christ" mentioned in the text. These terms are even placed side-by-side in verse 14. There is a relationship between Christ's broken body and Christian maturity. During the Lord's Supper, we show our partaking of Christ's blood with the wine (grape juice), picturing our redemption and the purgation of sin, and the partaking of His body through the broken bread, picturing the life we live after His example.

> *"I beseech you therefore, brethren, by the mercies of God, that ye present your bodies a living sacrifice, holy, acceptable unto God, which is your reasonable service. And be not conformed to this world: but be ye transformed by the renewing of your mind, that ye may prove what is that good, and acceptable, and perfect, will of God."* Romans 12:1-2

A bit more will be said about this in the comments under v. 20.

> *"But this man, after he had offered one sacrifice for sins for ever, sat down on the right hand of God; From henceforth expecting till his enemies be made his footstool."* vv. 12-13

Christ's priestly duty will continue until the day when the last enemy will be defeated (see comments under 1:13 in this commentary).

> *"For by one offering he hath perfected for ever them that are sanctified. Whereof the Holy Ghost also is a witness to us: for after that he had said before, This is the covenant that I will make with them after those days, saith the Lord, I will put my laws into their hearts, and in their minds will I write them; And their sins and iniquities will I remember no more. Now where remission of these is, there is no more offering for sin.* vv. 14-18

Here the author returns to the New Covenant. "To us" is further proof that the 'New Covenant' referred to here is with the ethnically Jewish, as that is who is writing and being written to. This return to the covenant would make sense because everything the author has said since the last mention of the covenant (9:1) provides the basis upon which the New Covenant is possible (including the establishment of the new *testament*!). It was taken from Jeremiah 31:33 but would not have been possible at that time because Christ had not come and died. The only thing wanting now is the return of God's attention to His chosen people, which cannot happen until His church is taken out of the way in the rapture. He will turn to her, and after much tribulation, she will turn to Him.

The law being put into their hearts mirrors Psalm 40:8, which the author had just quoted in verse 9. This has not happened yet.

Regarding *"their sins and iniquities will I remember no more."* This refers to the New Covenant, and therefore, to Israel specifically; yet it does the same thing for us. He has promised to 'forget' our iniquities. How can an omniscient Being forget? God's forgetfulness has no true human parallel; it is the best that human expression can muster. When a person truly forgives another, they no longer deal with that person according to the offense. We cannot really 'forgive and forget,' as the offense still causes pain. We choose to sacrifice the satisfaction of our feelings in order to maintain the relationship. If you do not, the person isn't forgiven. Forgiveness implies the perpetuation of the relationship. God's choice to "remember no more" is somehow related, though it involves His infinite nature, and is therefore likely to remain beyond our understanding.

Verse 18 is another reiteration of the finality of Christ's work. Its remission of sins is the only one, and it is final. This verse sets the stage for the coming exhortation, the second to last of the book.

> *"Having therefore, brethren, boldness to enter into the holiest by the blood of Jesus, By a new and living way, which he hath consecrated for us, through the veil, that is to say, his flesh; And having an high priest over the house of God; Let us draw near with a true heart in full assurance of faith, having our hearts sprinkled from an evil conscience, and our bodies washed with pure water." vv. 19-22*

If the book of Hebrews was a sermon, the doctrinal portion being wrapped up, our 'preacher' now turns to application.

We have already discussed 'boldness.' It is not arrogance. It is confidence in Christ's work. We should still approach God in the knowledge that He is utterly holy.

> "It must never be forgotten that the Gospel, with all its freedom and grace, does not modify in the slightest degree the character of God as holy, just, and true. In these respects the revelation of the new covenant

is identical with the old. While we have 'entrance,' it is into the 'holiest.'"[155]

Because of the work of Christ that the author has been describing, he exhorts his readers to (1) draw near (2) with a true heart (3) and full assurance. This is possible because (1) the heart has been sprinkled, and (2) the body washed with pure water.

The drawing near is the urging to progress in Christ-to mature as a Christian. The opposite is to "neglect so great salvation" (2:3), to "harden...your hearts" (3:8), to "fall away" (6:6), "draw back" (vv. 38-39). Drawing near is the goal that the author is aiming to push his readers toward.

The sprinkling of the blood to a clean conscience has been addressed, but what of this washing with pure water? Is it baptism? Is it the 'washing of the water by the word (Ephesians 5:26)?' We know that Christian baptism doesn't purify anything. Furthermore, have you ever seen anyone get baptized in 'pure water?' It cannot be baptism. Though the purifying effect of God's Word is real, we are talking about things Christ's work accomplished for us that allow us into God's presence. The author is also talking to Jewish Christians, using Old Testament typology that they would immediately recognize. There were washings in that system. The sacrifices were washed, and the priests were washed. We find our most direct representation in the latter. The work of Christ facilitated what the Old Testament priest

---

[155] Griffith Thomas, *Go On*, p. 137.

accomplished by washing their bodies-outward sanctification. The priests washed their bodies so that they might draw near to serve. What is pictured here is inward *and* outward cleansing. Our outward sanctification is important for we are to draw near to God, not for ourselves only, but on behalf of others. Unlike our inward sanctification, which guarantees access to God through prayer, our outward sanctification can hinder our effectiveness in relation to others (I Peter 3:7, for example).

The washing of the sacrifices during the consecration of the priests (Exodus 29) preceded their burning as a 'sweet savour' offering to God. This pictures a life of total consecration and worship to God, exemplified perfectly by Christ, the High Priest, and sought after in the lives of His children, the priesthood of believers. One cannot have true consecration without being clean

Having "a true heart" is what God has been after since the beginning. Israel, as long as they had a tabernacle or temple, continued to offer sacrifices; but their sacrifices-though according to the Law-would not be accepted by God. They offered them without "a true heart." This is one of the weaknesses of that Law, as stated earlier. Now that the Law, as well as everything that went along with it, has been satisfied in Christ, men and women, Jew and Gentile, regardless of station, situation, or geographic position, and regardless of age, can "draw near" to Christ. This may be what was referred to in the conversation between Jesus

Christ and the Samaritan woman at the well of Sychar:

> *"Jesus saith unto her, Woman, believe me, the hour cometh, when ye shall neither in this mountain, nor yet at Jerusalem, worship the Father. Ye worship ye know not what: we know what we worship: for salvation is of the Jews. But the hour cometh, and now is, when the true worshippers shall worship the Father in spirit and in truth: for the Father seeketh such to worship him. God is a Spirit: and they that worship him must worship him in spirit and in truth."* John 4:21-24

Lest the Christian be tempted to think that, since he or she may worship anywhere, attending church physically is optional, verse 25 is forthcoming.

The phrase "full assurance of faith" is interestingly placed. It is absolute proof that the book of Hebrews *does not* teach that one can lose salvation for how could they have full assurance without believer's security? You cannot be sure of God's acceptance of your worship unless your salvation is sure. Like the other security passages in Hebrews, it is ignored by commentators who are of this persuasion.

> *"Let us hold fast the profession of our faith without wavering; (for he is faithful that promised;) And let us consider one another to provoke unto love and to good works: vv. 23-24*

"Let us..." is what is known as a hortatory subjunctive, meaning the author gives a rallying cry that includes himself once again (total of 12 times in the book), proving that the exhortations are for saved people. They must be exhorted to worship, because salvation does not guarantee it, and to hold fast their profession because doing so is no more a given than worship. They are challenged to be faithful because God is faithful. They are once again pushed toward making sure their outward performance matches their inward reality. Notice the passage says to "hold fast the profession," not 'hold fast our faith.'

The passage says to "consider (or be considerate of) one another to provoke unto love and good works:" Again, these are not automatic for the Christian, and they are the reason for the Holy Spirit's insertion of the next verse:

> *"Not forsaking the assembling of ourselves together, as the manner of some is; but exhorting one another: and so much the more, as ye see the day approaching."* v. 25

We are not told to assemble so that we may merely provoke one another. We have a local community of redeemed believers who meet to worship God, through the Spirit, because of His Son, and to encourage one another to good works. This is what is known to New Testament Christianity as 'fellowship.' Fellowship, in the Scriptural sense isn't getting together and talking about whatever comes to mind. It isn't 'hanging out.' These things are fine in their place, but 'fellowship' has a purpose for the church. Our fellowship was meant to be 'gospel-centered' with Christ as its basis. Notice that fellowship is almost always attached to something:

"...the fellowship of his Son Jesus Christ our Lord." I Corinthians 1:9

"...the fellowship of the ministering to the saints." II Corinthians 8:4

"...your fellowship in the gospel..." Philippians 1:5

"...fellowship of the Spirit,..." Philippians 2:1

"...the fellowship of his sufferings,..." Philippians 3:10

Church members should be like family, but the *"assembling of ourselves together"* is for the purposes stated in these verses. The reason for this is that we need encouragement. We need each other's encouragement. If the assembly is forsaken, there is no one to provoke to good works; no one to exhort. This is why online church can never really replace meeting in person. We need each other. We need church. Don't forget, the context of this exhortation is 'drawing near!'

On a doctrinal note, some dispensationalists believe that the application of the book of Hebrews is to Jewish people after the Rapture of the church. If this is true, what an odd place to put instructions to the church!

The "day approaching" has been variously designated as: the Rapture of the church (Newell, Wuest) day of the Lord (Greene), Christ's return (Ironside, Gaebelein, Barclay), earthly judgment

(Griffith Thomas, Hobbs, Pentecost), judgment seat of Christ (Constable). This writer agrees with the Rapture view for these reasons: (1) It is established that the instructions given are for the church,[156] making the Rapture of the church the day we are looking for. (2) The 'day of the Lord' comes as a thief in the night (I Thessalonians 5:2). The "children of the day" (5:5) are not overtaken by it but look for His appearing in the clouds (the 'day of the Lord' is not the Rapture).[157]

> "This Hebrews passage is the counterpart to Romans xiii. 11, 12, 'Now is our salvation nearer than when we believed: the night is far spent, the day is at hand.' No one but a monster could regard the coming day of wrath as a hope. But the coming of Christ is the true hope of the people of God in every age."[158]

Christ's return is partially right-it depends on what the one saying it means. The Rapture is included, but is only the first phase. Verse 37 supports either interpretation. It certainly cannot be earthly judgment (the siege on Jerusalem), because these believers would escape that by

---

[156] The church in every age lives in view of the Rapture. This is a doctrine known as 'imminency,' where the Rapture could happen at any time.

[157] See the Chapter entitled "Pinpointing the Day of the Lord" from Stauffer, Douglas D., and Ray, Andrew B. *One Book Rightly Divided-Prophetic Edition* (McCowen Mills Publisher & LTB Publications, 2018), pp. 583-589.

[158] Anderson, *Types*, p. 85.

following the author's instructions. Those that did not are warned once again:

> *"For if we sin wilfully after that we have received the knowledge of the truth, there remaineth no more sacrifice for sins, But a certain fearful looking for of judgment and fiery indignation, which shall devour the adversaries. He that despised Moses' law died without mercy under two or three witnesses: Of how much sorer punishment, suppose ye, shall he be thought worthy, who hath trodden under foot the Son of God, and hath counted the blood of the covenant, wherewith he was sanctified, an unholy thing, and hath done despite unto the Spirit of grace? For we know him that hath said, Vengeance belongeth unto me, I will recompense, saith the Lord. And again, The Lord shall judge his people. It is a fearful thing to fall into the hands of the living God."* vv. 26-31

This passage is dark and downright scary. It talks about willfully sinning after receiving the knowledge of the truth. How many of us have sinned willfully after salvation? Because of its ominous feel and pronouncement of divine judgment, it is used to support the idea that a believer can lose his/her salvation. Despite the joy with which some run to such a horrible belief, this verse is a great defense for the doctrine of eternal security. How? It says that Jesus is the only sacrifice for sin (v. 26)! One would have to totally ignore everything that has come before this verse to think such a Sacrifice to be insufficient to secure eternal redemption!

Yet the passage obviously warrants further explanation. Two options are being presented: (1) resting in Christ as sufficient for salvation and sanctification, or (2) knowing these things and still turning belligerently away.

> "The wilful sin here warned against was turning back to Judaism, that religion which Christ by His coming had fulfilled. It was to set up again 'the first tabernacle'- the place of service of sacrificing priests, and thus to deny that the way into the holiest was open. And this is to tread under foot the Son of God, to treat His blood as common-no better than that of calves and goats, and to do despite to the Spirit of grace."[159]

> "Their turning back to Judaism gave proof that they were ignorant of the very rudiments, 'the first principles of Christ,' which Judaism taught (chap. v. 12; vi. 1)"[160]

The author does not say that the "sorer punishment" was a given, only that the offender should be thought worthy of it. Yet a fiery indignation did come upon those who turned back (if any did). In verse 27, the fiery indignation was coming for 'the adversaries.' Those who turned back would face the same judgment (and did). They went down *with* the adversaries.

---

[159] Anderson *Types*, p.78.
[160] Ibid, p. 79, n.

"…but as for that house, God had for certain long ago doomed it to the fire; and now that fatal day was come, according to the revolution of the ages:"[161]

Josephus gives an extended account of the siege and burning of the Temple. It reads like a horror film.

The problem with receiving advanced revelation from God is that now you are responsible for it. While these Jewish believers had been ignorant, they may have enjoyed some grace, but now they have no excuse.

"For unto whomsoever much is given, of him shall be much required: and to whom men have committed much, of him they will ask the more." Luke 12:48b

"But call to remembrance the former days, in which, after ye were illuminated, ye endured a great fight of afflictions; Partly, whilst ye were made a gazingstock both by reproaches and afflictions; and partly, whilst ye became companions of them that were so used. For ye had compassion of me in my bonds, and took joyfully the spoiling of your goods, knowing in yourselves that ye have in heaven a better and an enduring substance. Cast not away therefore your confidence, which hath great recompence of

---

[161] Josephus *The Wars of the Jews* Chapter IV, section 5, taken from *The Works of Josephus* (Hendrickson Publishers, 1985), p. 580.

reward. For ye have need of patience, that, after ye have done the will of God, ye might receive the promise. For yet a little while, and he that shall come will come, and will not tarry." vv. 32-37

This is a reminder of the journey these people had been through since coming to Christ. They were not only persecuted for their supposed apostatizing from the faith (Judaism), but for befriending and helping others that had apostatized. They had liquidated some of their own treasure to help the author of Hebrews while he was in jail. These trials, while unpleasant, are put in perspective by not only what disobedience would bring, but by the reward that the coming of Christ would bring. Just like the earthly tabernacle had an even 'truer' substance in the heavenlies, so their reward someday will be 'truer.'

"Lay not up for yourselves treasures upon earth, where moth and rust doth corrupt, and where thieves break through and steal: But lay up for yourselves treasures in heaven, where neither moth nor rust doth corrupt, and where thieves do not break through nor steal: For where your treasure is, there will your heart be also."
Matthew 6:19-21

"But as it is written, Eye hath not seen, nor ear heard, neither have entered into the heart of man, the things which God hath prepared for them that love him."
I Corinthians 2:9

Many of us have sacrificed and are sacrificing some things in order to serve God and be faithful to Him. To those we say:

"Cast not away therefore your confidence, which hath great recompence of reward. For ye have need of patience, that, after ye have done the will of God, ye might receive the promise. For yet a little while, and he that shall come will come, and will not tarry." Hebrews 10:35-37

We have reached the end of this part of the exhortation, and before embarking upon our survey of the well-known 'hall of faith,' let the reader be encouraged to keep in mind all that Christ has done so that we may enter the very presence of God, and to not neglect the privilege and the responsibility to do so.

"Under the law, it was death to go within the veil, under grace, it is death not to do so."[162]

Worship and prayer only once a week, with the pastor leading us by the hand is a sure recipe for an anemic Christian life. It will lead to discouragement at best, and disillusionment at worst. Remember the words of the songwriter:

Take time to be holy, speak oft with thy Lord;
Abide in Him always, and feed on His Word.
Make friends of God's children, help those who are weak,

---

[162] Moody, D.L. *Notes From My Bible* (Jernigan Press), p. 142.

Forgetting in nothing His blessing to seek.

Take time to be holy, the world rushes on;
Spend much time in secret, with Jesus alone.
By looking to Jesus, like Him thou shalt be;
Thy friends in thy conduct His likeness shall see.

Take time to be holy, let Him be thy Guide;
And run not before Him, whatever betide.
In joy or in sorrow, still follow the Lord,
And, looking to Jesus, still trust in His Word.

Take time to be holy, be calm in thy soul,
Each thought and each motive beneath His control.
Thus led by His Spirit to fountains of love,
Thou soon shalt be fitted for service above.
William D. Longstaff

"Now the just shall live by faith: but if any man draw back, my soul shall have no pleasure in him. But we are not of them who draw back unto perdition; but of them that believe to the saving of the soul." vv. 38-39

Though mentioned in many times in the book of Hebrews (this is the 6th of 30 total), faith is the key word. This verse (38) is the continuation of a reference to Habakkuk 2:3-4. It is a turning point in the 'sermon' that is Hebrews, and the emphasis now shifts from Christ as the superior Person, to faith as the superior principle. This follows every Christian's experience where the illumination of Christ is met by faith. It is God's prescribed progression, and this author's desire. It matches what we find in the book of Galatians:

228

> *"This only would I learn of you,*
> *Received ye the Spirit by the works of the law,*
> *or by the hearing of faith? Are ye so foolish?*
> *having begun in the Spirit, are ye now made*
> *perfect by the flesh?"* Galatians 3:2-3

Salvation comes through faith, and now the author of Hebrews, like Paul (coincidence?), urges perfection by faith.

This seemingly obscure text (Habakkuk 2:3-4) by a lesser-known minor prophet is used elsewhere in New Testament scripture, all three references coming through one author in particular: the apostle Paul. This lends further weight to the hypothesis that Paul authored this opus, as well as the others. Even if this is not true, the Holy Spirit ties them together in an astonishing way:

> "…this letter is the last of a series of three epistles forming together a divinely inspired commentary on one Old Testament text, namely Habakkuk 2:4, 'The just shall live by faith.' Romans expounds the first two words and shows who alone are 'the just' before God. Galatians continues the wondrous story and explains how the just 'shall live.' Having begun in the Spirit they are not to be made perfect by the flesh, but they live by the same faith that justifies. Now Hebrews completes the story, expounding the last two words, showing that it is 'by faith' God's

pilgrim people walk through this world to His praise and glory."[163]

If the letter to the Hebrews is a sermon, Habakkuk 2:4 is its text.

Some-to the point of exhaustion by now-have taken the second half of verse 38 as another statement of the inability of God to secure salvation for those who 'turn back.' The text is straightforward; it means what it says.

> "Christians can live by faith and please the Lord, or they can turn away and displease Him."[164]

A cognate verse is I Thessalonians 4:1:

> *"Furthermore then we beseech you, brethren, and exhort you by the Lord Jesus, that as ye have received of us how ye ought to walk and to please God, so ye would abound more and more."*

This verse, like the whole of Hebrews, is in the context of Christian maturity. There are multitudes of professing Christians living today who have decided to disobey God and arrest their Christian growth. These we exhort to repentance while there is still time, so they may stand before God unashamed and have 'somewhat to offer.' Verse 39 also addresses those who "draw back into perdition." Perdition is used to describe not only unbelievers, but conscious rejecters of God. In

---

[163] Ironside, H.A. *Hebrews and Titus*, p. 9.
[164] Lane, *Hebrews*, p. 147.

each case they are given a clear choice between God and evil, and they choose evil. The author is careful to say that believers are a separate group.

HEBREWS CHAPTER 11

". . . you have struck me as with roses." – Obadiah Holmes after 30 lashes with a whip[165]

"Now faith is the substance of things hoped for, the evidence of things not seen." Hebrews 11:1

This verse has often been described as definitional.[166] The flowery language can obscure the sense if the reader does not pause to meditate, for this is a deeper statement than first appears. It should be known that the 'hope' in this verse is in the same sense as the other usages in this letter (3:6; 6:11,18,19; 7:19). It is not a wish, or a longing that something might happen, but a confidence in something God has promised. This book is constantly and strongly urging its readers to bring their behavior in line with the promises of God. If they do not, it is because they lack faith.

Faith gives substance to the promises of God. We who look for this hope have staked our very lives and eternal futures on it. We raise our children in accord with it. We plan our lives around it. We base our decisions on it.

The *"evidence if things not seen"* is the present acquisition, by faith, of real future events and blessings.

---

[165] Grady, William P. *What Hath God Wrought* (Grady Publications Inc., Knoxville, 1996), p. 87.

[166] See, for instance, Morgan, *Triumph*, p. 20. Some disagree, such as Lane, p. 149.

"Faith confers upon a spiritual reality that we cannot see the full certainty of a proof of demonstration; . . . Christians know that realities which are not seen now will be seen in the future (italics removed)."[167]

"For by it the elders obtained a good report. Through faith we understand that the worlds were framed by the word of God, so that things which are seen were not made of things which do appear. By faith Abel offered unto God a more excellent sacrifice than Cain, by which he obtained witness that he was righteous, God testifying of his gifts: and by it he being dead yet speaketh. By faith Enoch was translated that he should not see death; and was not found, because God had translated him: for before his translation he had this testimony, that he pleased God. But without faith it is impossible to please him: for he that cometh to God must believe that he is, and that he is a rewarder of them that diligently seek him. By faith Noah, being warned of God of things not seen as yet, moved with fear, prepared an ark to the saving of his house; by the which he condemned the world, and became heir of the righteousness which is by faith. By faith Abraham, when he was called to go out into a place which he should after receive for an inheritance, obeyed; and he went out, not knowing whither he went. By faith he

---

[167] Lane, p. 149.

sojourned in the land of promise, as in a strange country, dwelling in tabernacles with Isaac and Jacob, the heirs with him of the same promise: For he looked for a city which hath foundations, whose builder and maker is God. Through faith also Sara herself received strength to conceive seed, and was delivered of a child when she was past age, because she judged him faithful who had promised. Therefore sprang there even of one, and him as good as dead, so many as the stars of the sky in multitude, and as the sand which is by the sea shore innumerable. These all died in faith, not having received the promises, but having seen them afar off, and were persuaded of them, and embraced them, and confessed that they were strangers and pilgrims on the earth. For they that say such things declare plainly that they seek a country. And truly, if they had been mindful of that country from whence they came out, they might have had opportunity to have returned. But now they desire a better country, that is, an heavenly: wherefore God is not ashamed to be called their God: for he hath prepared for them a city. By faith Abraham, when he was tried, offered up Isaac: and he that had received the promises offered up his only begotten son, Of whom it was said, That in Isaac shall thy seed be called: Accounting that God was able to raise him up, even from the dead; from whence also he received him in a figure. By faith Isaac blessed Jacob and Esau concerning things to come. By faith Jacob, when he was a dying, blessed both the sons of Joseph; and worshipped, leaning upon the top of his staff. By faith Joseph, when he died, made mention of the departing of the children of Israel; and gave commandment concerning his bones. By faith Moses, when he was born, was hid three months of his parents, because they saw he was a proper child; and they were not afraid of the king's commandment. By faith Moses, when he was come to years, refused to be called the son of Pharaoh's daughter; Choosing rather to suffer affliction with the people of God, than to enjoy the pleasures of sin for a season; Esteeming the reproach of Christ greater riches than the treasures in Egypt: for he had respect unto the recompence of the reward. By faith he forsook Egypt, not fearing the wrath of the king: for he endured, as seeing him who is invisible. Through faith he kept the passover, and the sprinkling of blood, lest he that destroyed the firstborn should touch them. By faith they passed through the Red sea as by dry land: which the Egyptians assaying to do were drowned. By faith the walls of Jericho fell down, after they were compassed about seven days. By faith the harlot Rahab perished not with them that believed not, when she had received the spies with peace. And what shall I more say?

for the time would fail me to tell of Gedeon, and of Barak, and of Samson, and of Jephthae; of David also, and Samuel, and of the prophets:" vv. 2-32

It is outside the purpose of the present study to examine each of the sixteen characters enumerated in this chapter. The main emphasis is faith, the purpose for which the author of Hebrews writes. In doing so, he displays Christ as superior to religion.

Verse 6 says that faith is what is required to please God. This has been the basis of man's dealings with God from the beginning. This writer has read some moderate dispensationalists who say that for Adam, as well as for those living during the Millenium, faith is not required at all because Jesus is physically present, and therefore salvation in those dispensations is based solely on works. It needs to be said that Adam's rebellion in garden of Eden was a conscious decision (I Timothy 2:14) based on a lack of faith. He loved his wife and did not want to live without her. What other options did he have? This writer would suggest that perhaps a greater faith in the nature of his God might have led him to make a different decision. Instead of trusting in the goodness of God, and placing Eve in His hands, he took the matter upon himself and made a calculated decision.

Those living during the Millenium have Christ before them, knowing *exactly* Who He is, and still choose Satan. Why would they do this? The rebellion of Revelation 20 mentions deception by Satan (v. 8). The deception is not disbelieving in

Who Christ is, but in His nature. Satan will likely use the ploy that has proven successful in past insurrections. In Isaiah 14, Satan makes a prideful attempt at God's throne. He may have had confidence in his ability, but he soon learned otherwise. His fall brought down a host of heavenly beings with him, as he convinced them of his plan. When he makes an attempt at Christ's earthly throne, he will take down a host of earthly beings. This time, he knows he cannot win. Winning isn't the point.

The Israelites at Kadesh Barnea had the pillar of cloud and fire, and the promise of God. They had seen Him! Because they lacked faith (Chapter 4), they failed to enter. When Christ 'came unto his own,' they were serving in the Temple, but without faith. Therefore, they 'received him not.'

Faith or belief has always been the answer. In the garden of Eden, Adam contracted a terminal, hereditary disease called sin. Good works are great, but they cannot remove this disease; they are tainted by it. Holy living only addresses the symptoms of this terminal illness; it cannot stop its effects. Mankind has dead blood and needs the cure, which is a 'blood transfusion'- living blood apprehended by faith alone, in Christ alone.

When Christ appeared on earth to His people in fulfillment of prophecy, He found them in a faithless situation. How did this happen?

God revealed to the Jews their religion. Its entire purpose was to look forward to Christ. As time went on, their religion and its law were added to. These added 'traditions (Matthew 15:3,6)' soon took on an authority of their own, and the Jewish people became devoted to the *practice* of Judaism, while losing sight of the *Person* Who gave it to them. The Jewish people that were practicing a strict Judaism, practiced it *without faith*. Remember Hebrews 10:6:

> *"In burnt offerings and sacrifices for sin thou hast had no pleasure."*

This is also the deciding factor in a more recent verse-10:38:

> *"Now the just shall live by faith: but if any man draw back, my soul shall have no pleasure in him."*

People of faith have pleasing God as their primary motivating factor (v.6) This is the purpose of faith-to please God, not to please us! It is a common refrain amongst so-called 'prosperity preachers' that the Christian life is for the benefit of the believer. This is the opposite of what we are called to. Christ did not die for Himself, He died for others. We are to follow Christ in crucifying our flesh for the benefit of others and to His glory. The outgrowth of the 'fruit of the Spirit' in Galatians 6 is for the same reason.[168]

---

[168] The pastor this writer grew up under put it in his special way. It goes something like this: "What if you were to plant an apple tree, and when you went to harvest the fruit, you found nothing but cores on the ground and heard the tree belch?! What would you do?" Silly perhaps, but a vivid picture of the self-centered Christian.

Today's Christian can just as easily slip into this exact trap. It is called 'legalism.' Holy living and standards are important, but we must not give 'traditions (false convictions, personal preferences)' the same authority as Scripture, and we must not get so caught up in the *practice* of Christianity that we lose sight of the *Person* of Christianity-Christ. There are those who are so 'holy' they can't get close enough to sinners to minister to them.

Notice that the first few characters precede the Law, and it is introduced in the middle of Moses, so to speak. There are the names of 14 men and 2 women, plus more of each listed indirectly (Amram and Jochebed, Moses' parents, for example). Newell noticed a progression in the first few names that parallels the Christian's experience in faith: Abel=salvation, Enoch=walking with God, Noah=judgment, and Abraham=promise.[169] Some highlights from the 'Hall of Faith' include:

<u>Abraham</u>- The passage clearly states his eyes were not on an earthly land. His eyes were on heaven. Next time you read Genesis 12-15, read it under this context.

<u>Jacob</u>- Jacob had to be taught to have faith. It was not until he learned to depend on God (Genesis 32) that his name was changed to Israel, and the course of his life began to change. Don't waste your life struggling with God over His will for you. Jacob was on his death bed before he blessed his children (Genesis 49).

---

[169] Newell, *Hebrews*, p. 378.

<u>Moses</u>- (1) His story of faith begins with his parents. If not for some things done in faith concerning Moses, we wouldn't have his story at all. Parents must, by faith, put things in place for the good of their children. Their ability to perform God's will to the fullest extent may depend on it. Remember that if you are a Christian parent, your first job is not to shield your children from every threat. It is to train them to follow God and enjoy His blessings. Putting Moses in a basket and floating him down the river had to have been scary, but it was God's will. (2) In verse 26, the Bible says that he esteemed *the reproach of Christ greater riches than the treasures in Egypt:"* This writer sees the Old Testament saints as 'looking forward to the Messiah.' *Every* Old Testament saint did since Genesis 3:15. God may have 'looked forward to the cross' in a manner of speaking, but the cross as a motif was unknown to everyone else. The wisest being in the universe outside of God didn't see it coming (I Corinthians 2:8.). (3) Verse 28 says Moses didn't fear Pharaoh's wrath. Do not think that this is a reference to Moses' flight to Horeb in Exodus 2:15:

> "Now when Pharaoh heard this thing, he sought to slay Moses. But Moses fled from the face of Pharaoh, and dwelt in the land of Midian: and he sat down by a well."

This was not a sterling moment of faith by Moses. Rather, the verse refers to Moses' bold return to face Pharaoh, which he did multiple times.

<u>Rahab</u>- Rahab holds a special place in this list because she isn't supposed to be here. In the Old Testament, God's 'elect' was Israel. Rahab was outside of the promise; she wasn't 'elect,' however God knew who she was and sent the spies to her home. Forget your past. Disregard feelings of not 'belonging.' Your fate isn't sealed until you take your last breath, or you trust in Christ.

> *"The Lord is not slack concerning his promise, as some men count slackness; but is longsuffering to us-ward, not willing that any should perish, but that all should come to repentance."* II Peter 3:9

One last note on the so-called 'roll call of faith.' This is a list of 'role models.' Are we to follow their example of righteousness? What example do we have? Abraham, Isaac, and Jacob were liars! Moses killed a man! Rahab was a prostitute! David was an adulterer *and* a murderer! Do we even need to talk about Samson? The example is not one of righteousness, but one of faith. Being righteous is important, but it's not the point here. Faith is what pleases God. So, no matter what your life looks like to this point, you can start today trying to please God by living, not a perfect life, because you cannot, but one of faith.

> *"Who through faith subdued kingdoms, wrought righteousness, obtained promises, stopped the mouths of lions, Quenched the violence of fire, escaped the edge of the sword, out of weakness were made strong, waxed valiant in fight, turned to flight the armies of the*

aliens. Women received their dead raised to life again: and others were tortured, not accepting deliverance; that they might obtain a better resurrection: And others had trial of cruel mockings and scourgings, yea, moreover of bonds and imprisonment: They were stoned, they were sawn asunder, were tempted, were slain with the sword: they wandered about in sheepskins and goatskins; being destitute, afflicted, tormented; (Of whom the world was not worthy:) they wandered in deserts, and in mountains, and in dens and caves of the earth. And these all, having obtained a good report through faith, received not the promise: God having provided some better thing for us, that they without us should not be made perfect." vv. 33-40

These are the annals of saints, known and unknown, and what they faced. Victory as well as defeat, death as well as resurrection, mocking as well as praise; this list spans the ages. From Stephen who was stoned (Acts 6 and 7), to today's Christians in places like China, India, Nigeria, North Korea, etc. The story of true Christianity is one of a faith that endures; looking toward something they had never seen, promised by Someone they have never met face-to-face. This is what the author of Hebrews is vehemently urging—a faith that endures. One that is not spoiled by good times or flushed out by bad times.

In the early 1st century in Rome:

"Mockery of every sort was added to their deaths. Covered with the skins of beasts, they were torn by dogs and perished, or were nailed to crosses, or were doomed to flames and burnt, to serve as a nightly illumination, when daylight had expired."[170]

In July 1555 at Smithfield:

"Bradford and Leaf went to the stake together, Bradford lying on one side of it to pray and Leaf on the other. After they had prayed silently for an hour, one of the sheriffs said to Bradford, "Get up and end this. The press of the crowd is great." They both got up. Bradford kissed a piece of firewood then the stake itself before addressing the crowd.

"England," he cried, "repent of your sins! Beware of idolatry. Beware of false antichrists. See they don't deceive you!" Then he forgave his persecutors and asked the crowd to pray for him. Turning his head to Leaf, Bradford told him, "Be at peace, brother. We will have a happy supper with the Lord tonight." Both men ended their lives without fear, hoping to obtain the prize for which they had long run."[171]

"And they overcame him by the blood of the Lamb, and by the word of their

---

[170] Tacitus, P. Conelius *The Annals and Histories* (Encyclopædia Britannica Inc., 1952), p. 168.
[171] Foxe, John *Foxe's Christian Martyrs* (Barbour Publishing, 2005), p. 129.

testimony; and they loved not their lives unto the death." Revelation 12:11

HEBREWS CHAPTER 12

"You cannot be, I know, nor do I wish to see you, an inactive spectator . . . . We have too many high sounding words, and too few actions that correspond with them." – Abigail Adams, to her husband John.[172]

"Wherefore seeing we also are compassed about with so great a cloud of witnesses, let us lay aside every weight, and the sin which doth so easily beset us, and let us run with patience the race that is set before us," Hebrews 12:1

Being "compassed" or surrounded by a great cloud of witnesses has been commonly interpreted to mean that the saints that have gone before-the ones enumerated in the last chapter up to today-are watching the current generation of faithful Christians, much like the audience at a track meet. This is not linguistically consistent. If you remember, the patriarchs of old "obtained witness (see 11:4)," therefore, the 'witnesses' are not the saints themselves, but the testimonies borne to them. It would be more proper to say that these testimonies are what compass us about. Our testimony of faith is one among thousands upon thousands of heroes and martyrs, and is meant to please God, giving more tooth to the urging of the author than if we were merely trying to impress those who have died in Christ.

---

172 McCullough, David G. *John Adams* (Simon & Schuster, New York, 2001), p. 17.

"It has been tempting to many writers to speak of our race being run in an arena surrounded by spectators, as though those that have passed on before are still interested in our welfare. But, however attractive the idea, it is impossible to derive from this passage."[173]

It is correct to make a distinction between "weight" and "sin." As to weight, and since the analogy is one of racing, we are best to picture weights like the runner does. Runners do not carry anything with them in the race. They wear the lightest possible clothing and the lightest possible shoes. Ankle weights may be good for training, but not for the race itself. The rule book does not disqualify heavy clothes or weights for obvious reasons. They are not illegal, but every runner understands that they put themselves at a distinct disadvantage by donning them. Just the same, the "weights" here are not sinful, but rather innocuous items that are out of their place. Things that, though not wrong, have taken the wrong place or have been given the wrong priority. A good job can be wonderful and provide a good life for one's family. It can also become a weight if it takes one out of church or gets them hooked on worldly things. Hobbies are similar. There is nothing wrong with a hobby until it takes up residence where the things of God once did. Doubtless the devil is behind car and hobby shows, football games, and kids' sporting events being held on the Lord's Day.

---

[173] Griffith Thomas *Go On,* p. 157.

Anything that gets in the way of serving God to the best of one's ability is a weight.

> "…a 'weight' is anything that hinders our spiritual growth and the effectiveness of our testimony."[174]

> "Some one is recorded to have asked whether a certain thing would do a personal harm, and the reply was given, 'No harm, if you do not wish to win.'"[175]

Sins that easily beset are against the rules of the race. They can get you disqualified (knock you out of the race). The author of Hebrews doesn't want his readers to allow 'besetting sins' to rule the day. If there is something that easily besets you, put some barriers in place that make it harder to fall for the next time it presents itself. David said, *"I will set no wicked thing before mine eyes:*(Psalm 101:3a)" His son Solomon said concerning the way of the wicked, "Avoid it, pass not by it, turn from it, and pass away *(Proverbs 4:15).*" It is the essence of what Christ was saying in Matthew 18:8-9: *"If thine eye offend thee…"* If you cannot control your conduct on a smartphone, something must be done (Though some believe they could sooner live without an eye than their smartphone).

Paul liked the race analogy. In fact, he used it in I Corinthians, Galatians, Philippians, and II Timothy (coincidence?). It is instructive for our purposes to view these briefly.

---

[174] Greene, *Hebrews,* p. 525.
[175] Griffith Thomas, *Go On,* p. 156.

"Know ye not that they which run in a race run all, but one receiveth the prize? So run, that ye may obtain. And every man that striveth for the mastery is temperate in all things. Now they do it to obtain a corruptible crown; but we an incorruptible. I therefore so run, not as uncertainly; so fight I, not as one that beateth the air: But I keep under my body, and bring it into subjection: lest that by any means, when I have preached to others, I myself should be a castaway." I Corinthians 9:24-27

The purpose of the Holy Spirit through Paul in this passage is not to put the Christian life in terms of competing.

"The idea of a race is generally competition; here it is only concentration of purpose, singleness of aim, intensity."[176]

One does not wander onto a course and find themselves in a race. One must qualify and enter, the goal of the race being victory. We entered a race when we were saved, and the prize is Christ. If you are running for any other reason, you will come short of the prize. This writer has heard some say they are running to win prizes in the Millenium. If this has been your mindset, your motives are incorrect. Paul sought to 'win Christ (Philippians 3:8),' to fulfill his calling in Christ (Philippians 3:14), and to win crowns (see I Corinthians 9:25 above), which will be cast at the feet of Jesus at

---

[176] Meyer, *Holiest*, p. 143.

His coronation (Revelation 4:10[177]). We don't run to glorify ourselves, but to glorify Christ (see comments under 11:6).

The Christian life is a race, but only one kind of race fits the analogy. It is a long-distance marathon. It is not a sprint or (God help!) a relay. It is easy to run a short distance. You can be out of shape and run a short distance. You can carry weights for a short distance. The Christian life is a long haul. Far too many Christians come out of the gate with great energy, only to fizzle out. The author of Hebrews is urging endurance.

The term 'patience' is used here. In arguably every case, the New Testament definition of 'patience' is endurance through suffering and is often found running alongside faith.

> "This means which we possess is no romantic thing; it is not something which lends us wings to fly over the difficulties and the hard places. It is that determination, unhasting and unresting, unhurrinying and yet undelaying, which goes steadily on, and which refuses to be deflected."[178]

---

[177] This writer is aware that only the 24 elders are said to cast their crowns. It is commonly held that this is our cue, and that we will quickly follow suit. This writer also believes that He that sits on the throne is also God the Father, with Christ at His right hand, Christ receiving the crown somewhere around Revelation 11:15, as He is seen in Revelation 14:14 wearing the crown as He 'cleans house' in preparation for the Millennium.

[178] Barclay, *Hebrews,* p. 196.

There are manifold reasons for encountering trials in the Christian life. One must not immediately assume the purpose of those trials to be that of discipline. When encountering a trial, we ought to examine ourselves to be sure we are not ignoring the convicting action of the Holy Spirit concerning our condition. If and once doubt is removed concerning personal sin, we must resign ourselves to the fact that God allows trials into our lives to make us better Christians; to fit us for service.

> *"And I will turn my hand upon thee, and purely purge away thy dross, and take away all thy tin:"* Isaiah 1:25

> *"Take away the dross from the silver, and there shall come forth a vessel for the finer."* Proverbs 25:4

Knowing this makes it possible for the Christian to achieve an attitude of thankfulness for trials. Can you imagine the immense witness to the Gospel as the unregenerate in our lives look on as we patiently bear trials with gratitude?

> *"That the trial of your faith, being much more precious than of gold that perisheth, though it be tried with fire, might be found unto praise and honour and glory at the appearing of Jesus Christ:"* 1 Peter 1:7

> *"Looking unto Jesus the author and finisher of our faith; who for the joy that was set before him endured the cross, despising*

the shame, and is set down at the right hand of the throne of God." v. 2

If the theme of Hebrews is "Christ is Superior," this may be its central verse. Jesus is the ultimate example of faith. Though it is difficult (if not impossible) to understand, Jesus seems to be described as having faith in Galatians 2:20. This faith finds its fulfillment in Christ's obedience to the Father in enduring the crucifixion, expecting that the Father would deliver to Him the "joy" mentioned in our present text. In other words, Christ believed the Father's promise. We are called to do the same; the difference being that we cannot have perfect faith.

Many have complained about the fact that the word "*our*" is not in 'the original (how would they know? We say, "Prove it; show us 'the original!'").' Faith as a concept needs no 'author' nor 'finisher.' Every man has faith in *something*. 'Our faith' is singular. It is based on the Faithful One. He pioneered it as described above, and that He is the "Finisher" of it will doubtless be revealed in glory. This is not the end of any other faith; only ours.

The current chapter begins the final warning or exhortation (see the table at the beginning of the comments under chapter 2) of the sermon we call Hebrews. The exhortation is to endurance, and the means of endurance is to look unto Jesus. Here, He is extolled as the superlative Example (or better 'ensample') of faith.

The failure to keep one's eyes on Christ is illustrated in the story of Peter's walk on the water. Peter, in faith, steps out onto the surface of the waves, until something happens:

> *"But when he saw the wind boisterous, he was afraid; and beginning to sink, he cried, saying, Lord, save me. And immediately Jesus stretched forth his hand, and caught him, and said unto him, O thou of little faith, wherefore didst thou doubt?"* Matthew 14:30-31

Peter became distracted by the tempest and took his eyes off the Savior. His lapse of faith caused him to sink. The analogy is clear-if the Jewish Christians take their eyes off Christ, they will be overwhelmed by their trials. This is the worry for our author, and the answer is to look to Jesus.

> "Looking to Jesus and Jesus alone. Looking to Him always and in all. In trial and trouble, as in joy and prosperity; in solitude and repose, as in company and business; in religious worship, as in daily life; -always, only, looking to Jesus."[179]

As a teenager attending driving school, this writer recalls the instructor saying, "You will end up where you look." She was teaching the students to place their eyes in the center of the lane they were in, and not at oncoming traffic or the scenery around them. A driver tends to drift toward the

---

[179] Murray, *The Holiest*, p. 483.

object of their attention. It was as good advice for a young driver as it is for a Christian at any age.

Because of the proximity of "the joy that was set before him" to "and is set down at the right hand of the throne of God.", Nearly every commentary consulted made the exaltation of Christ by God to His position there the "joy." This cannot be so, as He had that joy prior. One does not leave home for work because they look forward to coming home again, unless they gain something along the way (in this case, wages). There are two possibilities here. One is found in Wuest, which says that He traded the joy that was before Him in heaven to come to Earth and be crucified.[180] This is based on the meaning of the Greek word for "for" in the text. It is "ἀντί", or "anti" and it can mean "instead of." However, It can also mean "because of" which matches the traditional view more closely. If the latter is the case, and the 'joy' isn't simply returning to the Fasther's side, there must be something more to it. This writer believes the 'joy' to be His "bringing many sons to glory (2:10)." Newell comes through in this vein:

> "The joy of being the means of *letting out the heart of God* toward His creatures was **set before** Christ! When He bare men's sins and put them away, then the mighty river of *grace, pure grace,* from the *heart* of God, Who *delighteth in mercy*, could *pour forth*! (italics and bold letters his)"[181]

---

[180] Wuest, *Hebrews*, p. 215-216.
[181] Newell, *Hebrews*, p. 403.

God/Christ mourns over every lost sinner and rejoices over every found son to an extent we may never grasp the edges of.

> *"For consider him that endured such contradiction of sinners against himself, lest ye be wearied and faint in your minds."* Hebrews 12:3

"Consider Him!" This is the essence of the Christian life. He is the One we look to, the One we model our own lives after. We strive to follow His example in prayer, in submission, in service, in meekness, and in suffering.

> "The only aim that it is worthy of a man to live for, as his supreme and dominant one, is that he shall be completely moulded in character, disposition, nature, heart, and will into the likeness of Jesus Christ. . .the complete development of human character into the divine image, and the complete union of the human with the divine, is the aim that Christianity sets before us."[182]

Volumes could be written on the subject of 'consider Him,' yet for our purposes, the author has something specific in mind that he would have his readers consider, and that is the patient endurance of Christ through suffering. This suffering is described in the verse not as physical pain, but as the "contradiction of sinners against himself,".

---

[182] Maclaren, *Expositions*, 179.

"This contradiction began the moment He was born."[183]

Christ was continually faced by a contradiction, and that is that He was continuously subject to rejection and scorn by those whom He came to Earth to save.

A pastor stands week to week, after arduously digging bare-handed through the soil of God's word, pleading for the salvation and sanctification of a group of people who nod in assent, yet fail to use the tools handed them by him. He watches as they wander into sin and spiritual sterility, despite his ceaseless warning and exhortation. He is like the mother who, after a day of picking up careless laundry, cleaning thoughtless messes, and making thankless provisions labors over a hearty meal, only to have her children turn up their nose and refuse to eat. Sure, there are those few who really 'get it,' but these he thanks God for and moves on. It is the others that rob him of his sleep. Of the many pressures of the ministry, this must surely be the most frustrating and exhausting; but the one thing a pastor cannot do is to quit.

The experience of any Christian laborer is similar. Who among us has not been derided or had a door slammed against us while extending the offer of the Gospel?

---

[183] Greene, *Hebrews*, p. 532.

> *"Because the carnal mind is enmity against God: for it is not subject to the law of God, neither indeed can be."* Romans 8:7

> *"If the world hate you, ye know that it hated me before it hated you."* John 15:18

It is by considering in a detailed way the patient endurance of our Lord while He labored among us, that we draw fresh strength and encouragement to press forward through service and suffering.

> *"Ye have not yet resisted unto blood, striving against sin."* v. 4

The point here is that, although these Christians had suffered hostility and loss of property and relationships, they had not suffered to the degree that Christ had. We live at a time and place in the history of God's church where we suffer very little because of the Gospel. Yet II Timothy 3:12 says, *"Yea, and all that will live godly in Christ Jesus shall suffer persecution."* Not only should it be expected, but at this point, there is so very little that ought to deter us from enduring in the faith.

> *"And ye have forgotten the exhortation which speaketh unto you as unto children, My son, despise not thou the chastening of the Lord, nor faint when thou art rebuked of him: For whom the Lord loveth he chasteneth, and scourgeth every son whom he receiveth. If ye endure chastening, God dealeth with you as with sons; for what son is he whom the father chasteneth not?*

But if ye be without chastisement, whereof all are partakers, then are ye bastards, and not sons. Furthermore we have had fathers of our flesh which corrected us, and we gave them reverence: shall we not much rather be in subjection unto the Father of spirits, and live? For they verily for a few days chastened us after their own pleasure; but he for our profit, that we might be partakers of his holiness. Now no chastening for the present seemeth to be joyous, but grievous: nevertheless afterward it yieldeth the peaceable fruit of righteousness unto them which are exercised thereby." vv. 5-11

The author of Hebrews now moves into a brief discussion on what William Lane terms 'disciplinary sufferings.'[184] There are three categories of problems Christians face: (1) trial by God for discipline concerning direct disobedience, (2) that which occurs incidentally, which God allows for the shaping and bettering of the Christian, and (3) natural consequences caused by the Christian failing to pattern their life after Christ. Too often, we cause our own problems and then blame it on 'the enemy' or worse, on God. The 'disciplinary sufferings' being dealt with here are an amalgam of problems (1) and (2) above. Discipline involves everything from positive reinforcement to corporal punishment, therefore the analogy to the father-son relationship is fitting. Discipline is to be expected if we are indeed the sons (and daughters)

---

[184] Lane, *Hebrews*, 162.

of God. If there is never any discipline, something is wrong.

The author again references the Old Testament, this time Proverbs 3:11 and 12.

A father, if he is wise, will pay attention to the conduct of his child and respond appropriately. A child who is obstinate is likely to receive the full measure of justice, whereas a child who is immediately repentant may obtain mercy. A father who merely punishes his children is not practicing discipline. Likewise, God deals with us as children, but He does not 'punish' us. All the punishment we deserve was dealt upon Christ. The discipline that God allows is designed to drive us into His arms.

> "Punishment is the retribution for evil, and for the believer the punishment has already been received by the Messiah on the cross. Discipline, on the other hand, is moral training to conform the son to the expectation of the father."[185]

If you have sinned, your relationship with God has been affected. You are more likely to face silence than suffering. This is a time of introspection and confession. The more realistic the view of oneself, the brighter shines the glory of God. Viewing God in His rightful place causes one to remember the past blessings of God, which is how *the goodness of God leadeth thee to repentance* (Romans 2:4)."

---

[185] Fruchtenbaum, *Ariel's*, p. 173.

The sufferings the author of Hebrews is presenting are like the watchful training a child receives. A wise father may allow his child to experience hardship so that he may learn from it or become stronger. We, as Christians facing difficult times, need to remember three things: (1) God only disciplines those He loves, and (2) those that belong to Him, and (3) the discipline we receive as children of God can only ever be for our good to our maturity. If we forget these things, like the Christians to whom the author of Hebrews writes, we will fail to obtain God's intended benefit for us in the trial. The presence of suffering in our lives will bring about one of two things, depending upon our attitude toward them: (1) maturity with gratitude, or (2) falling away with bitterness (if you are bitter, you are out of God's will). Can you imagine being *thankful* for suffering?

> *"Behold, happy is the man whom God correcteth: therefore despise not thou the chastening of the Almighty:"* Job 5:17[186]

The intended benefits listed in the text are holiness and the fruits of righteousness (vv. 10 and 11). These results are the "pleasure" that God looks to when allowing these things into our lives. This helps us to understand this text and others. A good father takes no pleasure in chastening his child verbally or physically, but rather reaps pleasure when the chastening results in a positive behavioral change. The same is true for God. Thus,

---

[186] This writer is aware that Eliphaz's premise in Job 5 is flawed, but the principle here is nonetheless a true one.

we see that when the prophet says "Yet it pleased the LORD to bruise him (Isaiah 53:10a);" he means that God was pleased because He was looking forward to the *result* of Christ's bruising-the redemption of mankind.

> *"Wherefore lift up the hands which hang down, and the feeble knees; And make straight paths for your feet, lest that which is lame be turned out of the way; but let it rather be healed."* vv. 12-13

The author not only encourages his readers to take heart but admonishes them to encourage others also. The antecedent for verse 13 is verse 5. The chastening of the Lord, if received, will tend to maturity, righteousness, holiness, and now healing, whereas the fallout of a failure to receive it is fainting and falling out of the way. "That which is lame" cannot walk, and the believer's walk is the day-to-day devotional life he or she experiences when in fellowship with Him. It is your choice to "be turned out of the way," or to be "healed." God will not heal you until you make that choice (see discussion on 6:4-6). It is our job to encourage those that are not walking to begin again; to pick up where they left off.

> *"Follow peace with all men, and holiness, without which no man shall see the Lord: Looking diligently lest any man fail of the grace of God; lest any root of bitterness springing up trouble you, and thereby many be defiled;"* vv. 14-15

Peace is something that must be pursued constantly. It is mentioned here because a lack of concern for peace hinders the 'runner' as well as his fellows.

> "A fighting church or denomination is a denial before the world of all that for which the name of Christ stands. If Christ's people cannot live in peace among themselves, who can? (cf. Matt. 5:9)."[187]

Holiness is included here because compromise with the world or with sin is never God's means of accomplishing peace. Infighting within the church is a swift killer and will destroy those that are weak in the faith. A divided church is one that hampers the ministry of the Holy Spirit. God has promised to be present (Matthew 18:20), but He will not move.

Failing of the grace of God in verse 15 is identical to what Paul calls in Galatians "falling from grace (5:4)." It is turning from a dependence on grace for sanctification, to being dominated by legalism. It is a failure to "draw near (10:22)" and "find grace to help in time of need (4:16)." This is a follow-on from the intra-church relations discussion that began in verse 12. If a church loses focus on encouraging one another through trials, and seeking peace with holiness, their focus will turn to themselves, and legalism will develop. The legalist thinks himself holy because his love for God is greater or purer than that of others, proven by his extensive list of convictions. The legalist hums

---

[187] Hobbs, *Hebrews*, 126.

along fine until he enters a trial. He then looks on that brother who 'does not love God as much as he does (the one with less convictions),' and Satan has an open door to plant bitterness within his heart. This will lead to division, gossip, and resignation and "thereby many be defiled." With such an effective weapon, why would Satan not resort to it often? This is why the author warns vigilance.

Notice the stark contrast between "peace with holiness" and "root of bitterness springing up" and "many being defiled."

> *"Lest there be any fornicator, or profane person, as Esau, who for one morsel of meat sold his birthright. For ye know how that afterward, when he would have inherited the blessing, he was rejected: for he found no place of repentance, though he sought it carefully with tears."* vv. 16-17

These two verses display the culmination of a progression which started in the previous verses. The first step is failing of the grace of God or failing to appropriate grace when needed. Step two is the root of bitterness springing up. Up to now, the problem has been internal to the individual, but if not dealt with, it will infect others. The next is many being defiled, or the bitterness spreading to others as described above, and the final step is a rejection, repudiation, or resignation of one's Christian privilege and duty. Esau is typical of this condition.

Esau is not known for being particularly heinous concerning extramarital conduct. In fact, he married a Hittite (Genesis 26:34-35), then seeing that his parents did not approve, sought a wife that came from Abraham (Genesis 28:8-9). This appears to be an attempt at moving in the right direction, however misguided.

The problem for Esau was not physical fornication so much as spiritual fornication, which is the intention of our verse. Throughout the books of the prophets, Israel's idolatry is described in this way. Is it coincidental that the gods Israel sought were sensual in nature? Like Israel, Esau traded faith for fleshly satisfaction. This narrative is found in Genesis 25:29-34. Esau was in full knowledge of what his birthright entailed and traded it to satisfy the affliction of hunger. Is there a better parallel to the situation the first century Jewish Christians faced in their time? They could either seek a temporary reprieve from persecution by returning to the old way or they could continue persisting in faith. Like Esau, had they given in, they would have traded their spiritual blessings for momentary relief. This is a continual danger for today's child of God. There is constant pressure to yield to the flesh instead of to the Spirit, the direct consequence is the forfeiture of the blessings which God longs to give. Remember Bob Jones Sr.'s plea: "Never sacrifice the permanent on the altar of the immediate."

Two interpretational ditches are present here, dug by sincere men with spades of theological bias. The one is to say that Esau wanted to repent but could not because God would not allow him. The other ditch is to say that because

Esau committed the unpardonable sin and lost his salvation, and so can we. Can these things be true? The author of Hebrews is trying to draw a parallel between the current exhortation and Genesis 25:29-34. It behooves the reader to read both carefully. Esau did not throw away salvation, but inheritance. Not sonship, but the blessing of the firstborn. He was not repentant concerning his profaneness but sought his father's repentance concerning the blessing without dealing with the sin that caused him to lose it in the first place. This is suddenly sounding like Hebrews 6:4-6, where God will not allow the Christian to mature while he or she is rejecting known truth. So, we see that this warning again concerns something other than salvation and has nothing at all to do with God using 'sovereign grace' against people.

> *"For ye are not come unto the mount that might be touched, and that burned with fire, nor unto blackness, and darkness, and tempest, And the sound of a trumpet, and the voice of words; which voice they that heard intreated that the word should not be spoken to them any more: (For they could not endure that which was commanded, And if so much as a beast touch the mountain, it shall be stoned, or thrust through with a dart: And so terrible was the sight, that Moses said, I exceedingly fear and quake:) But ye are come unto mount Sion, and unto the city of the living God, the heavenly Jerusalem, and to an innumerable company of angels, To the general assembly and church of the*

firstborn, which are written in heaven, and to God the Judge of all, and to the spirits of just men made perfect, And to Jesus the mediator of the new covenant, and to the blood of sprinkling, that speaketh better things than that of Abel." vv. 18-24

This is a continuance of the positive side of the Hebrews coin, the negative being the warnings of the book, the positive being the admonition to draw near because of Who Christ is. Being no longer under the dispensation of the frightful rigidity of the Law, but under the new dispensation of abundant and welcoming grace, the believer has no excuse for not calling upon that grace the moment it is recognized that it is needed. Identify the root of bitterness and dig it out before it springs up and manifests itself as a plant bearing noxious and poisonous fruit. There is so much at stake.

The allusion to "the church of the firstborn" in verse 23 is a problem for those who believe the book of Hebrews to be written primarily to tribulation age Jewish believers. If Hebrews is written to a people living after the rapture of the church, what is the church doing there? It cannot be dismissed by making the word 'firstborn' a reference to Jews.[188] Though it is true that Israel is referred to as God's firstborn (Exodus 4:22, for instance), the entire passage argues against

---

[188]Ruckman, *Hebrews*, 393. Replacement theology is accused of repeatedly making Israel into the Church to force Scripture into their theological framework. Here moderate dispensationalists make the Church Israel for the same purpose.

'firstborn' in this instance being a reference to ethnic Israelites. Rather, it describes moving from law unto grace, from God dealing primarily with the Jewish people, to dealing with the body of Christ.

> *"For by one Spirit are we all baptized into one body, whether we be Jews or Gentiles, whether we be bond or free; and have been all made to drink into one Spirit."*
> I Corinthians 12:13

The *"church of the firstborn"* has three possible meanings based on the term 'firstborn.' Either it is the portion of the church that is ethnically Jewish,[189] for they are God's firstborn, or to Christ, which is the "firstborn of every creature (Colossians 1:15)," and the "firstborn from the dead (Colossians 1:18)." The third possibility is that "firstborn" applies to all those born again (Romans 8:29). One reason to prefer this interpretation is that the author of Hebrews is currently dealing with the treatment of sons (vv. 5-11), and with Esau and what they stand (and stood) to gain and lose. Remember that it is the firstborn that receives the inheritance. All three meanings, however, have something to commend them to us.

There is a comparison between the physical mount Sinai, also called Horeb, and the spiritual mount Sion. Each description is sevenfold.[190]

---

[189] Fruchtenbaum, *Ariel's*, p. 182.
[190] Griffith Thomas, *Go On*, p. 165-166.

"In contrast with Sinai comes this reference
to Mount Sion; instead of terrors are glories;
instead of the material, the spiritual; instead
of distance, access."[191]

The Old Testament law was given at mount
Sinai and was a hard taskmaster, whereas the 'law
of liberty (James 1:25)' comes down from mount
Zion, and the King's subjects delight in it. If this
sounds like relief, we should temper our excitement
by remembering the holiness of God; that we take
no advantage of His mercy and neglect that law of
liberty. Just like the warnings that have come
before, there is the reality of Christ, followed by the
consequences of departing from it.

This introduces the final warning passage
and includes the final 'better.' Christ's blood speaks
"better things than that of Abel." We see the
parallels between Christ and Abel; like Christ, Abel
is described as righteous (Hebrews 11:4), a
shepherd (Genesis 4:2), both were slain of their
brethren (Genesis 4:8), God had respect to their
offerings (Genesis 4:4), and the blood of each bear
testimony (Hebrews 11:4, again). These are just a
few of the similarities. Yet Christ's blood bears a
much greater testimony. Abel's blood could only
testify against Cain and his was the first in a string
of deaths which would testify against Israel. In
Matthew 23:27-36, our Lord gives an 'A-to-Z'
account, and it ends with the current generation of
the time, for they would shed one more Man's
blood for the same reason as the rest. They didn't

---

[191] Ibid, p. 166.

have to, but they did, and it testified against them. We have access to that very same blood, and in the courtroom of God will hear it testify as to whether we availed ourselves of it or not. This was also the blood which brought in the New Testament and will bring in the New Covenant when He comes the second time.

> *"See that ye refuse not him that speaketh. For if they escaped not who refused him that spake on earth, much more shall not we escape, if we turn away from him that speaketh from heaven: Whose voice then shook the earth: but now he hath promised, saying, Yet once more I shake not the earth only, but also heaven. And this word, Yet once more, signifieth the removing of those things that are shaken, as of things that are made, that those things which cannot be shaken may remain. Wherefore we receiving a kingdom which cannot be moved, let us have grace, whereby we may serve God acceptably with reverence and godly fear: For our God is a consuming fire."*
> vv. 25-29

The *"him that speaketh"* is God in the person of the Lord Jesus Christ, bringing full-circle a motif introduced in the very first verses of this book:

> *"God, who at sundry times and in divers manners spake in time past unto the fathers by the prophets, Hath in these last days spoken unto us by his Son, whom he*

*hath appointed heir of all things, by whom
also he made the worlds;"*

It was God Who spoke at Sinai and shook the earth. It is God Who will yet speak, this time to shake both heaven and earth. This is a reference to Haggai 2:6 and brings the modern reader into eschatology. The fire of God will once again fall in judgment. Verse 29 is a quotation from Deuteronomy 4:24 and has implications for this epistle's audience in the time it was written and for us today. The acceptance of the blood of Christ for salvation shields the believer from eternal damnation. Sadly, the inverse is also true for the unbelieving rejector. The blood of Christ is also appropriated by the believer on a continuing basis, for it is by this blood that we maintain our relationship with God through Christ. God's desire in saving us is that we take advantage of the application of His blood by faith for fellowship with Him, so that He can work through us to accomplish His will for us. So many fail to maintain this consistently, and it is everything that falls outside of this that will be consumed in the fires of judgment. The first century Christians faced judgment with the adversaries (10:27), as well as the loss of reward in the life to come. We face the fires of God's judgment as described in I Corinthians 3:11-16, as well as the possibility of temporal judgment as described in the following verse (I Corinthians 3:17). God opened the floodgates of mercy and grace, which flow still today from the heavenly mount, yet the author of Hebrews wants to remind us to approach God with no less reverence than those who stood at the foot of Sinai, or even Moses, God's chosen representative who trembled and quaked. Approach Him we must and avail ourselves of that grace, for great is the testimony against us if we do not.

As we have seen throughout this study, Christ has done everything possible to bring us to this point. His blood has fully reconciled us to God, made the way of holiness available to us, and, as described in the 'heavenly Sion' portion, seated us in 'heavenly places' with Him (Ephesians 2:6)! Rejoice in this, while maintaining Godly fear and reverence, and remain ever watchful. Remember how this section began-with failing to apprehend free grace, to a root of bitterness, and then to outright rejection.

HEBREWS CHAPTER 13

"He may be somewhat diffuse and circuitous in his representations, but it will be found, that, in the end, he comes round to his case, and makes every thing bear upon the verdict which he desires." – William Shedd, of a lawyer[192]

> *"Let brotherly love continue."* Hebrews 13:1

As we come into the final chapter of this great book, we come across language that could easily be lifted out and dropped into any of Paul's epistles without a hint of disjointedness. The thirteenth chapter reads like one of his letters and stands as a kind of postscript to the material that precedes it. The author turns from theological explanations and tough exhortations to a collection of practical instructions.

> "It should be recalled that someone said that Hebrews begins like an essay, proceeds like a sermon, and ends like a letter. Chapter 13 is the *letter*."[193]

These instructions begin with the encouragement to "let brotherly love continue." The author obviously felt it needed to be said.

> "Brotherly love is evidence of heavenly citizenship. If we do not love our brethren

---

[192] Shedd, William G.T. *Homiletics and Pastoral Theology* (Scribner's, New York, 1867), p. 246.
[193] Hobbs, *Hebrews,* p. 133.

whom we have seen, how can we love God whom we have not seen? It is worthy of notice that Jesus said to His disciples, 'By this shall all men know that ye are my disciples, if ye have love one to another.' (John 13:35)."[194]

Brotherly love within a church is in danger on many fronts. The first is mere negligence. When someone makes the decision to join a local assembly, they enter into covenant between themselves and the other members of that body. The familial bonds that exist between us and other believers exist as a consequence of the Spirit that lives within us, but the relationship to other members of our own local church is far closer, and we are called into a fellowship that requires determination and effort to maintain. We, in essence, join a family.

A second danger is that of offense. Believers are to have grace one with another. We are to be conscious of how we might offend others in the church, while at the same time having understanding toward those whose actions might be taken as offense. This fights the battle against division from both sides.

A third danger is that of self-righteousness. As described in the comments about legalism under 12:15, self-righteousness begins with a desire to please God, but that goal is often lost sight of, the end being prideful disdain for those who are perceived as less 'holy.' For the Hebrew

---

[194] Greene, *Hebrews*, p. 574.

Christians who were raised in such a strict environment as orthodox Judaism, the temptation to become a 'Christian Pharisee' was continuously present.

> "The very fact that they took their religion as seriously as they did was in one sense a danger."[195]

This does not mean we are not at risk as well. The more avid the Bible student, the more expert a 'heresy hunter' they become. We should deal gently with those who are earnest but erring, as well as those who are weak in the faith. We should be ever ready to "restore such a one (Galatians 6:1)" who messes up or falls by the way. Remember 12:12:

> *"Wherefore lift up the hands which hang down, and the feeble knees;"*

Brotherly love is something to be pursued, the key being our interest in the spiritual well-being of those with whom we are in local fellowship. We are to intercede earnestly for one another when we enter the throne room of God in prayer. It is difficult to despise someone when you are praying for them to a God Who loves them, on the basis of Him Who gave His very life for the both of you.

> *"Be not forgetful to entertain strangers: for thereby some have entertained angels unawares."* v. 2

---

[195] Barclay, *Hebrews,* p.217.

This is a call to hospitality. It is tempting to emphasize the latter half of the verse because of the mystery it holds concerning angels, but this does not seem to be the primary force of the verse. This is the thirteenth mention of angels in this book, the same Greek word being used each time (ἄγγελος, or we would say 'angelos'). Many make reference to Abraham hosting the angel of the Lord and His companions in Genesis 18. The reader should be aware that the text allows for the meaning of 'angels' in this verse to be that of 'pastors' as in Revelation 1 and 2. In each case, the 'angels' or 'messengers' are on a mission, and the host accommodates them in that mission. This recalls the seeming purpose of angels themselves as described in this very book (1:7). The emphasis seems to be on having a tendency toward hospitality, for only God knows what good can arise out of such a disposition.

> *"Remember them that are in bonds, as bound with them; and them which suffer adversity, as being yourselves also in the body."* v. 3

To remember those who are detained for the Gospel's sake (a rare occurrence in today's American church, though perhaps not so in the near future), is to be in a shared state of mind, for we could just as easily be as they are. Whenever God 'remembers' someone in Scripture, it is the onus for the action it introduces, in other words, God 'remembers' by attending to those whom He remembers. For instance,

"And God remembered Rachel, and God hearkened to her, and opened her womb." Genesis 30:22

Also, when God 'remembered' Noah, he brought about the end of the Flood, etc., etc. Therefore, the implication is to 'remember' a fellow saint by taking action: lifting them up in prayer, as well as in whatever other way possible. Visits, and gifts (as allowed by law) are a supreme encouragement.

"Marriage is honourable in all, and the bed undefiled: but whoremongers and adulterers God will judge. Let your conversation be without covetousness; and be content with such things as ye have: for he hath said, I will never leave thee, nor forsake thee." vv. 4-5

A lot of preaching could be done out of these two verses. It would be cogent to relate the two together as they speak to our modern American culture. Perhaps the two biggest hazards for the American Christian, because they so permeate our culture, is prosperity and sensuality. The pressure to cave to both is immense. One will draw you away from ministry, while the other will destroy it. Today's Christian *must* make a steadfast determination to avoid both to follow Jesus. James warns us of the danger of split loyalty:

"A double minded man is unstable in all his ways." James 1:8

> *"Draw nigh to God, and he will draw*
> *nigh to you. Cleanse your hands, ye sinners;*
> *and purify your hearts, ye double minded."*
> James 4:8

You cannot serve God while being unfaithful to your spouse. It is impossible to be spiritual while maintaining a pornography habit (yes, pornography is fornication!).

A conversation (one's manner of living) without covetousness is free of jealousy over the prosperity of others. One who is in pursuit of God has no time to 'keep up with the Joneses.' One whose eyes are on Christ (12:2 "Looking unto Jesus...") won't even notice the Joneses.

> *"Set your affection on things above,*
> *not on things on the earth."* Colossians 3:2

The basis for this perspective comes at the end of verse 5: "I will never leave thee, nor forsake thee." One who has Christ has all they need. It is also the greatest verse in the entire book concerning eternal security. Christ has promised that He will never leave or forsake us, and this verse comes *without conditions*. If one could lose salvation, Christ would be forsaking them just when they need Him most!

This idea (eternal security) is not merely a New Testament theme, but one that is found throughout the Old Testament.

> "The former reference is
> not found in so many words in the Old
> Testament, but is an obvious

adaptation of several passages (Gen. 28:15; Deut. 31:6; Josh. 1:5; Isa. 41:17)."[196]

"So that we may boldly say, The Lord is my helper, and I will not fear what man shall do unto me." v. 6

This is from Psalm 118:6. Man can take anything from you except your soul, which belongs to God. This is how this verse relates to the two which precede it.

"And fear not them which kill the body, but are not able to kill the soul: but rather fear him which is able to destroy both soul and body in hell." Matthew 10:28

"Remember them which have the rule over you, who have spoken unto you the word of God: whose faith follow, considering the end of their conversation." v. 7

The idea of 'rule' here is not one of rank. Those who 'rule' over the church do not 'lord over it.' This English word is used in the New Testament in that sense, but the context makes it obvious; for instance, Mark 10:42 states:

"But Jesus called them to him, and saith unto them, Ye know that they which are accounted to rule over the Gentiles exercise lordship over them; and their great ones exercise authority upon them."

---

[196] Griffith Thomas, *Go On*, p. 174.

Incidentally, the underlying Greek word is different, in this case "ἄρχω" or "arco" as in archangel, etc. For our verse in Hebrews, however, the underlying Greek is "ἡγέομαι" or "hegeomai" from which we get the English word 'hegemony,' which is associated with the jurisdiction of a ruler. The Greek root of this Greek word often has nothing to do with impressing one's authority on anyone, but rather one of providing a standard or example by which they are led. This is the idea behind the Bible's third employment of the English word 'rule,' backed by the Greek word "κανών" or "kanon," from which we get canon, which means 'rule' or 'standard.' This is the 'rule (canon)' by which the pastors or elders 'rule (hegeomai),' in II Corinthians 6:10 and 15, Galatians 6:16, Philippians 3:16, etc. This is more important than it might appear because the abuse of verses like this one has made allowance for unscriptural hierarchy within the church throughout the ages. The idea of 'ruling' here is one of setting the standard for those of the congregation to follow. You can see from the verse that, like the heroes of chapter 11, it is their faith that we are called to follow. This expression occurs two more times in this chapter (13) and is used in the same sense all three times. These rulers are most likely the current leadership of the church (as they are to be saluted in verse 24), and their 'rule' should follow this sense. Remember I Peter 5:1 and 2:

> *"Feed the flock of God which is among you, taking the oversight thereof, not by constraint, but willingly; not for filthy lucre, but of a ready mind; Neither as being lords*

*over God's heritage, but being ensamples to
the flock."*

"...considering the end of their conversation."
This writer believes that the sense here is that the
readers ask themselves the 'why' of the manner of
life their examples have adopted. People risk
becoming dissatisfied or even bitter with their
pastor when they lose sight of why he does what
he does. If he is right with God, his whole purpose
is to bring his congregants to maturity in Christ,
and for this we are grateful. A lack of appreciation
is the first step to becoming bitter against the man
of God.

*"Jesus Christ the same yesterday,
and to day, and for ever."* v. 8

This verse is often quoted as a statement on
the immutability of Christ, which it absolutely is,
however the reason this statement occurs here has
everything to do with perseverance. The program
or dispensation has changed; Christ has not. The
way to the Holiest of All, as well as its location has
changed, Christ has not. These Christians no longer
enter through a picture of Christ, but through
Christ Himself. This sets the table for the verses
that follow.

*"Be not carried about with divers and
strange doctrines. For it is a good thing that
the heart be established with grace; not with
meats, which have not profited them that
have been occupied therein. We have an
altar, whereof they have no right to eat which
serve the tabernacle. For the bodies of those*

beasts, whose blood is brought into the sanctuary by the high priest for sin, are burned without the camp. Wherefore Jesus also, that he might sanctify the people with his own blood, suffered without the gate. Let us go forth therefore unto him without the camp, bearing his reproach. For here have we no continuing city, but we seek one to come. By him therefore let us offer the sacrifice of praise to God continually, that is, the fruit of our lips giving thanks to his name. But to do good and to communicate forget not: for with such sacrifices God is well pleased." vv. 9-16

As many of the New Testament letters show, the early churches were just as subject to false doctrine as today's churches are.

> "'What is false doctrine?' asked the teacher. 'False doctoring,' answered one little boy in the class, 'is when the doctor gives the wrong stuff to sick folks.'"[197]

False doctrine usually enters when false teaching obtains purchase within the church. The book of Galatians especially deals with the attempts of some to bring works into sanctification, and Hebrew Christians had approached God this way throughout their lives. It must have been very hard for them to train their minds to reorient themselves to the grace that had been shed abroad at Calvary, but they had to do it, for the temptation

[197] Naismith, A. *A Treasury of Notes, Quotes, and Anecdotes* (Baker Book House, Grand Rapids, 1976), p. 79.

to stray from would have been perpetual. As stated before, convictions are good to have, but they are not the foundation; *grace* is. Even those among us who did not come from a works-based religion often try to earn God's love or acceptance with our service to Him. As also stated before, our works should flow out of our love for Him, not out of an effort to buy His love. Would you rather your children perform their chores joyfully, simply because they are happy to be part of a loving family, or because they are in constant fear that they will lose your approval?

The "right to eat" which we have is the right to partake of Christ, granted to us as the royal priesthood. To really understand what the author is getting at in this section (9-16), we need to keep in mind the system that Christ is superior to, and what its process shows typologically. The altar was inside the Temple, and this is where the priest's portion was consumed. The blood was taken and applied to the altar. The bodies of the beasts were then taken outside to be burned as our text says. This process is found in Exodus 28 and 29. This portion is from 28:32-34:

> *"And Aaron and his sons shall eat the flesh of the ram, and the bread that is in the basket, by the door of the tabernacle of the congregation. And they shall eat those things wherewith the atonement was made, to consecrate and to sanctify them: but a stranger shall not eat thereof, because they are holy. And if ought of the flesh of the consecrations, or of the bread, remain unto*

the morning, then thou shalt burn the remainder with fire: it shall not be eaten, because it is holy."

What did this mean for the first century Hebrew Christians? To mature, they had to make a clean break from Jewish Temple service, and by going 'outside the camp,' they would save themselves from the literal, physical judgment that was to shortly fall upon Jerusalem by emperor Titus. They would also subject themselves to persecution.

"But before all these, they shall lay their hands on you, and persecute you, delivering you up to the synagogues, and into prisons, being brought before kings and rulers for my name's sake." Luke 21:12

"As many as desire to make a fair shew in the flesh, they constrain you to be circumcised; only lest they should suffer persecution for the cross of Christ." Galatians 6:12

"Yea, and all that will live godly in Christ Jesus shall suffer persecution." II Timothy 3:12

What does it mean for us? The passage in Exodus from which the author takes his example concerns the consecration of the priests. The priests are typical of the saved in the church. Notice that a 'stranger' was not allowed to partake. An unsaved person cannot be consecrated to Christ. This is for saved people, just like the rest of the book, and has to do with maturity. We approach God for fellowship-to 'partake of Christ,' then what follows is the fruit of that, the completion of the consecration process, the total commitment to God. Our lives are to be totally consumed by Him, leaving nothing for ourselves to hold. If there is a part of your heart that is held back from God, you have not reached maturity.

The location of the final stage of consecration is "without the camp," where we will be "bearing his reproach." A person who is in an apostate church that teaches a corrupt gospel cannot remain a member and reach maturity. Christians find they must often remove themselves from certain living conditions, circles of friends, and workplaces, as they greatly hinder spiritual growth (remember 12:1). We must be willing to face the hardship that comes with being 'outside the camp.'

What follows is a call to "go forth therefore unto him without the camp, bearing his reproach." As stated before, when a sacrifice is burnt, it is a picture of total consecration. Jesus gave His body completely, without reservation, to the will of the Father, and is our example. The call to 'go without the camp' had special meaning for the Hebrew Christians as 'the camp' was all they had ever known, and those who did not leave would face severe judgment. Our example is the same. There will come a time in every Christian's life where the situation will cause them to either hide their faith or leave the proverbial camp and bear some reproach for the name of Christ, with heaven in mind. Just like Abraham in chapter 11 verse 10, we too look "for a city which hath foundations, whose builder and maker *is* God."

> "We cannot stop in the condemned city; we must be outside its walls. Our Lord went out of the city to die, and we must go without the camp to live."[198]

This kind of separation requires strength, and the author urges his readers to draw it from the knowledge of the destination to which they are headed. Jerusalem was destined to fall, and we, like they, look for an eternal city: New Jerusalem!

Just because there are no longer animal sacrifices does not mean the need for sacrifice has ended. We, as believers, are called to live our entire lives sacrificially, following the pattern of Christ, vis-à-vis Romans 12:1:

> "*I beseech you therefore, brethren, by the mercies of God, that ye present your bodies a living sacrifice, holy, acceptable unto God, which is your reasonable service.*"

This means extends to every area of life. We are to give both money and time sacrificially, but also to offer the sacrifice of praise; not only because He is worthy, but because it benefits those around us. Our children need to hear us extoll the Lord. The lost of our community need to hear how good He is. Our brethren will be encouraged if we open our mouths in praise.

---

[198] Spurgeon, Charles H., *Spurgeon's Verse Exposition of Hebrews* (Expansive Commentary Collection, Kindle edition), p. 208.

"Obey them that have the rule over you, and submit yourselves: for they watch for your souls, as they that must give account, that they may do it with joy, and not with grief: for that is unprofitable for you. Pray for us: for we trust we have a good conscience, in all things willing to live honestly." vv. 17, 18

This is similar to verse 7, but with the added burden to pray for those in leadership, remembering that they will someday have to give account of their stewardship to God. This writer has heard Christians boldly demand their pastor give account to them, all the while forgetting that they will answer to God for their own conduct. The call to submission is voluntary, but the result is the profit of the submitted, not the one submitted to. Remember that submission isn't true until it is tested. It doesn't manifest itself until the wills of the parties diverge. Even the immature church member will celebrate the pastor while he operates according to their plan. When he makes a decision they don't like, they may go so far as to thirst for his destruction.

"Woe unto the world because of offences! for it must needs be that offences come; but woe to that man by whom the offence cometh!" Matthew 18:7

"If the spirit of the ruler rise up against thee, leave not thy place; for yielding pacifieth great offences." Ecclesiastes 10:4[199]

"But I beseech you the rather to do this, that I may be restored to you the sooner." v. 19

This statement is where the idea comes from that the author was incarcerated at the time of writing. His desire is to minister among them once again.

"Now the God of peace, that brought again from the dead our Lord Jesus, that great shepherd of the sheep, through the blood of the everlasting covenant, Make you perfect in every good work to do his will, working in you that which is wellpleasing in his sight, through Jesus Christ; to whom be glory for ever and ever. Amen." vv. 20, 21

These two verses are considered a benediction, and they sum up the purpose of the entire book in a tight, concise, and extremely beautiful fashion.

It is God, through Christ that is the emotive force behind any good that comes from our lives, but His choice is to operate only through hearts that are completely yielded to Him.

---

[199] This writer is aware of the context of this verse, but the principle makes good advice, nonetheless.

> *"And I beseech you, brethren, suffer the word of exhortation: for I have written a letter unto you in few words. Know ye that our brother Timothy is set at liberty; with whom, if he come shortly, I will see you. Salute all them that have the rule over you, and all the saints. They of Italy salute you. Grace be with you all. Amen."* vv. 22-25

A modern equivalence may run: "I'm begging you, please put up with a little hard preaching..."

"...in few words." There are 5,038 in the Greek Textus Receptus. When expressed in English, there are 6,913. For this to be few words, one's measure might have to be the one the Beloved Disciple used in John 21:25:

> *"And there are also many other things which Jesus did, the which, if they should be written every one, I suppose that even the world itself could not contain the books that should be written. Amen."*

In other words, there is so much that could be written about Christ's work and how it completes everything that they knew, that a mere 6,913 words can only scratch the surface!

The report of Timothy's release from prison makes the author contemporary and on close terms with him. The author anticipates his own release, and to see the letter's recipients shortly. The author passes on a greeting from the saints in Italy (from where it could be assumed he is writing), and in doing so, closes this inspired letter.

If there is any closing message, it is this: No system of religion can bring you to the place where God longs to bring you. You must allow it, or you will die, and Christ-the Superior High Priest- is your means and avenue of entrance.

> "If we are to do God's will we must have the spirit of Him who said, 'I come to do Thy will, O Lord; and Thy law is within My heart.' Let us open our hearts to Him; let us seek for Him to enter in. And then, 'the God of peace, that brought again from the dead the Lord Jesus, that great Shepherd of the sheep, through the blood of the everlasting covenant, shall make us perfect in every good; to do His will, working that which is well-pleasing in His sight, through Jesus Christ."[200]

---

[200] MacLaren, *Expositions,* p. 350.

Excursus 1

What does 'moderate dispensationalism' teach about the book of Hebrews?

Moderate dispensationalism holds that Old Testament saints could lose their salvation. They further hold that during the Tribulation (Jacob's trouble), God returns to the dispensation of the Law, and so the way of salvation returns to that of the Old Testament and so can once again be lost. They believe that since the book of Hebrews has primary application to early Jewish Christians, and Tribulation Jews (to which this writer agrees), the book of Hebrews teaches that salvation can be lost (to which this writer disagrees). As concerns Hebrews, the primary challenges to this view are: (a) The book of Hebrews describes Christ as a better High Priest. If He did not secure the salvation of the readers of this book, just how is Christ better than what came before? (b) It runs counter to progressive revelation. Moderate dispensationalism depends on progressive revelation for the changes in the way of salvation as the ages pass.[201] At the time of both the writing of Hebrews, and the Tribulation, Christ's finished work has been revealed, and cannot be unrevealed—and—if the works of Tribulation saints contribute to their salvation, Christ's work was not finished. (c) Every stage of progressive revelation (each dispensation) brings a fuller understanding of God and brings believers closer to Christ. A

------

[201] Walker, David, *Rightly Dividing the Bible Volume One* (WestBow Press, 2018), Loc. 984, Kindle edition.

return to the dispensation of Law would be a step backward. (d) In Acts 15:5-10, Peter is arguing against a group of Pharisees in the Jerusalem church who are teaching that the law of Moses must be kept. Peter says in verse 10 that the law of Moses was a yoke that their fathers were unable to bear, and that to put the disciples under it would be to tempt God. Yet moderate dispensationalism would add even more burdens to this yoke:

> "If the Lord comes and you remain behind, then start working like a madman to get to Heaven, because you're going to have to. You have entered a period of time called "the Great Tribulation," and the plan of salvation in the Tribulation is faith in Jesus Christ plus your own good works."

> "You must keep the Ten Commandments (all of them, Ecclesiastes 12:13), keep the Golden Rule (I John 3:10), give your money to the poor, get baptized, take up your cross, hold out to the end of the Tribulation, wait for Jesus Christ to show up at the Battle of Armageddon, and be prepared to die for what you believe. In the Tribulation, you cannot be saved by grace alone like you could before the Rapture."[202]

What is the purpose for doing this? This does not sound like a God Who "is not willing that any should perish (II Peter 3:9)" or that "will have all men to be saved (I Timothy 2:4)." (e) Finally, the

---

[202] Ruckman, Peter S., *Millions Disappear, Fact or Fiction?* (Self-published by P.R.S., 1989), 20.

whole book of Hebrews is attempting to convince Jewish Christians to forsake Old Testament Judaism for New Testament Christianity. How can it be used to teach that Jews in the Tribulation should go back to Old Testament Judaism? While it's true that there seems to be a temple in operation during the tribulation, this doesn't necessarily mean God has any more respect for the Jewish sacrifices than He did when Hebrews was written.

Excursus 2

Does the weight of evidence within the book of Hebrews indicate salvation can be lost?

A list-though probably not exhaustive-of verses that are 'explained' by the faith-plus-works system is given in the afterword to a moderate dispensational commentary on the book of Hebrews and runs as follows: Hebrews 1:2, 6, 14; 3:6, 14; 4:2, 11; 6:4-6; 10:26-31; and 11:10, 14, 39.[203] That is 19 verses in total. The verses that could not be included if salvation was dependent on works are 1:3, 14; 2:9-15, 17; 3:1, 19; 4:2-3, 6, 10, 14-16; 5:6-7, 9-10; 6:1, 10-20, 7:3 (arguably), 11, 15-28; the entirety of chapter 8 (13 verses); 9:11-15, 24-28; 10:1, 5, 10, 12, 14-18, 21-22, 38-39; 11:39-40; 12:2, 5-11, 15, 22-24, 28; and 13:5-6, 8-9, 12, 15-16, 20. The total is over 100. A few of the standouts are: 2:3: "so great salvation." If the faith-plus-works model is true, salvation would be more difficult to obtain than ever; 6:19: "Which *hope* we have as an anchor of the soul, both sure and stedfast,"; 7:25 ". . .he is able also to save them to the uttermost that come unto God by him, seeing he ever liveth to make intercession for them."; 9:12 ". . .having obtained eternal redemption *for us*."; and perhaps best of all, 13:5 ". . .I will never leave thee, nor forsake thee." The book of Hebrews is about "just men made perfect," and a few difficult verses should never be used to overthrow the entire intention of the book in which they are found.

---

[203] Ibid, 444.

Chapter 13 poses a problem for moderate dispensationalists:

> "The author of the last chapter is undoubtedly Paul while the other twelve chapters contain material of such a nature that to this day no one can nail down the author for certain. If I were pressed for an answer I would say the first twelve chapters were written while Paul was in Arabia, and...
> I presume Paul wrote the last chapter sometime after Acts 20."[204]

This author later says that the first 12 chapters were written before Acts 7.[205] If moderate dispensationalism is true, and Paul wrote the first 12 chapters, then added the 13th at a later date, he was either ignorant, careless, outright negligent, or out to confuse people. By adding a postscript to this letter, Paul effectively placed a stamp of approval on its contents. We now have Paul circulating a letter during a dispensation in which it should have been considered heresy. This is confusion, of which God is not the author.

---

[204] Ruckman, *Hebrews,* preface xvii.
[205] Ibid, 149-150.

BIBLIOGRAPHY

Anderson, Sir Robert, *Types In Hebrews*. Grand Rapids: Kregel Publications, 1978.

Barnes, Albert. *Notes on the New Testament-Hebrews.* Grand Rapids: Baker Book House, 1951.

Barclay, William. *The Letter to the Hebrews.* Philadelphia: The Westminster Press, 1957.

Boettner, Lorraine, *Studies in Theology.* Philadelphia: The Presbyterian and Reformed Publishing Company, 1947.

Broadus, John A. *The History of Preaching*. New York: A.C. Armstrong & Son, 1889.

Chafer, Lewis Sperry. *Systematic Theology.* Dallas Theological Seminary, 1947.

Charnock, Stephen. *The Works of Stephen Charnock, Volume Five.* Banner of Truth Trust, 2021.

Church of Jesus Christ of Latter-Day Saints. "Angel Moroni." https://www.churchofjesuschrist.org/study/history/topics/angel-moroni?lang=eng. Accessed 4-15-2023.

Church, J.R. *Hidden Prophecies in the Psalms.* Prophecy Publications, 1986.

Clarke, Adam. *Clarke's Commentary Volume V., Matthew-Acts.* Abingdon-Cokesbury.

Clegg, Brian. *The God Effect.* New York: St. Martin's Press, 2006.

Constable, Thomas. *Notes on Hebrews,* 2023. Kindle.

Copan, Paul and Craig, William L. *Creation Out of Nothing.* Baker Academic, 2004.

Dillow, Joseph C. *The Reign of the Servant Kings.* Schoettle Publishing, 1992.

Edersheim, Alfred. *The Temple-It's Ministry & Services.* Religious Tract Society.

Emlen, S., "Charlie" Garret and Voitenko, Sergio. *Hebrews.* SuperiorWord.org, https://study-pdfs.s3.amazonaws.com/hebrews-commentary-rev2.pdf, 2022.

Encyclopedia Britannica. "Quran." Qur'an | Description, Meaning, History, & Facts | Britannica. Accessed 4-15-2023.

Evans, William. *The Great Doctrines of the Bible.* Chicago: Moody Press, 1974.

Exell, Rev. Joseph S. *The Biblical Expositor-Hebrews Vol. 1.* London: James Nisbet & Co.

Flavel, John. *The Fountain of Life.* American Tract Society.

Foxe, John. *Foxe's Christian Martyrs.* Barbour Publishing, 2005.

Fruchtenbaum, Arnold G. *Ariel's Bible Commentary-The Messianic Jewish Epistles*. Ariel Ministries, 2005.

Gaebelein, A.C. *The Annotated Bible: Phil-Hebrews.* New York: Our Hope, 1917.

Gantz, Jeffrey, trans. *The Mabinogion.* New York: Barnes & Noble, 1996.

Geisler, Norman. "God Knows All." In *Predestination & Free Will,* Edited by David and Randall Basinger, pp. 63-84. InterVarsity Press, 1986.

Grady, William P. *What Hath God Wrought.* Knoxville: Grady Publications Inc. 1996.

Greene, Oliver B. *The Epistle of Paul the Apostle to the Hebrews.* Greenville: Gospel Hour, Inc., 1965.

Habershon, Ada R. *A Study of the Types.* Grand Rapids: Kregel Publications, 1973.

Haldeman, I.M. *The Tabernacle-Priesthood and Offerings.* New Jersey: Revell, 1925.

Hobbs, Herschel. *Hebrews-Challenges to Bold Leadership.* Scripture Truth Book Co., 1971.

Hodge, Charles. *Systematic Theology, Volume 1-Theology.* Peabody: Hendrickson Publishers, 2020.

Ironside, Harry A., *Studies in the Epistle to the Hebrews and the Epistle to Titus.* New York: Loizeaux Brothers, Inc., 1932.

Jehovah's Witnesses. "Who is Michael the Archangel?" https://www.jw.org/en/bible-teachings/questions/archangel-michael/. Accessed 4-15-2023.

Josephus, Flavius. *The Works of Josephus.* Peabody: Hendrickson Publishers, 1985.

Kent, Homer A., Jr. *The Epistle to the Hebrews.* Grand Rapids: Baker Book House, 1983.

Kittel, Gerhard, ed. *Theological Dictionary of the New Testament.* Grand Rapids: Wm. B. Eerdman's Publishing Company, 1964.

Lane, William L. *Hebrews-A Call to Commitment.* Peabody: Hendrickson, 1985.

Lenski, Richard C. H. *The Interpretation of the Epistle to the Hebrews and the Epistle of James.* Augsburg Publishing House, 1963.

Lewis, C.S. *Mere Christianity* (Macmillan Publishing, 1952.

Lockyer, Herbert. *All the Men of the Bible.* Grand Rapids: Zondervan Publishing House, 1975.

MacArthur, John. "Hebrews 6 and Loss of Salvation." https://www.gty.org/library/questions/ QA198/hebrews-6-and-the-loss-of-salvation, accessed 7-21-2023.

MacArthur, John. "The Blood of Christ." https://www.gty.org/library/sermons-library/80-44/the-blood-of-christ.

MacLaren, Alexander. *Expositions of Holy Scripture, Volume 10-II Timothy, Titus, Philemon, Hebrews, James, Ephesians.* Grand Rapids: Wm. B. Eerdmans, 1952.

McGee, J. Vernon *Thru the Bible – Vol. V.* Thomas Nelson, 1983.

Meyer, F.B., *The Way Into the Holiest.* Grand Rapids: Zondervan Publishing House, 1950.

Moody, D.L. *Notes From My Bible.* Jernigan Press.

Morgan, G. Campbell. *The Triumph of Faith.* New Jersey: Revell, 1944.

Morris, Henry *The Genesis Record.* Grand Rapids: Baker Book House, 1976.

Morris, Leon. *Hebrews-Revelation,* vol. 12 of *The Expositor's Bible Commentary.*

McCullough, David C. *John Adams.* New York: Simon & Schuster Inc., 2001.

Murray, Andrew *The Holiest of All.* New Jersey: Fleming H. Revell Company.

Naismith, A. *A Treasury of Notes, Quotes, and Anecdotes.* Grand Rapids: Baker Book House, 1976.

Newell, William, *Hebrews Verse by Verse.* Iowa Falls: World Bible Publishers, 1947.

Penrose, Roger *The Emperor's New Mind.* Oxford University Press, 1989.

Pink, Arthur W. *An Exposition of Hebrews.* Grand Rapids: Baker Book House, 1974.

Plummer, Alfred. *An Exegetical Commentary on the Gospel According to St. Matthew.* Robert Scott, 1909.

Rawlinson, George, trans. *The History of Herodotus.* Taylor Publishing Company, 1956.

Rowley, J.B. "Exposition of Hebrews Six 'An Age-Long Battleground'" *Bibliotheca Sacra*, July

1937. https://www.galaxie.com/article/bsac94-375-05.

Rokser, Dennis M. *Salvation in Three Time Zones.* Grace Gospel Press, 2013.

Ruckman, Peter S. *Millions Disappear, Fact or Fiction?* Self-published, 1989.

Ruckman, Peter S. *The Book of Hebrews.* Self-published, 1986.

Ryrie, Charles C. *Dispensationalism Today.* Chicago: Moody Press, 1965.

Santayana, George The Unknowable-Oxford Lectures on Philosophy 1910-1932. Kessinger Whitefish, 1924.

Saphir, Adolph. *The Epistle to the Hebrews: An Exposition-volume 1.* New York: Loizeaux Brothers, 1946.

Saphir, Adolph. *The Epistle to the Hebrews: An Exposition-volume 2.* New York: Loizeaux Brothers, 1946.

Shedd, William G.T. *Homiletics and Pastoral Theology*. New York: Charles Scribner & Co., 1867.

Spurgeon, Charles H. *Spurgeon's Verse Exposition of Hebrews.* Expansive Commentary Collection. Kindle.

Stauffer, Douglas D., and Ray, Andrew B. *One Book Rightly Divided-Prophetic Edition.* McCowen Mills Publisher & LTB Publications, 2018.

Swenson, Richard A. *More Than Meets the Eye.* NavPress, 2000.

Tacitus, P. Cornelius. *The Annals and Histories.* Encyclopædia Britannica, Inc. 1952.

Thomas, W.H. Griffith, *Let Us Go On.* Grand Rapids: Zondervan Publishing House, 1944.

Tozer, A.W. *A.W. Tozer: An Anthology.* Christian Publications, 1984.

Tyndale, William. *Works of William Tyndale Volume I.* Banner of Truth Trust, 2010.

Unger, Merrill F. *Unger's Bible Handbook.* Chicago: Moody Press, 1966.

Vance, Laurence M. *The Other Side of Calvinism.* Revised Edition. Vance Publications, 2014.

Walker, David. *Rightly Dividing the Bible Volume One.* WestBow Press, 2018. Kindle.

Walvoord, John F. *The Millennial Kingdom.* Grand Rapids: Zondervan, 1959.

Watterson, Bill. *There's Treasure Everywhere.* Andrews and McMeel, 1996.

Wiersbe, Warren W. *The Bible Exposition Commentary-volume 2.* Victor Books, 1989.

Wuest, Kenneth S. *Hebrews in the Greek New Testament.* Grand Rapids: Wm. B. Eerdmans Publishing Company, 1947.

ABOUT THE AUTHOR

The author was born in 1985 into a faithful Christian home and saved at the age of 7 under the ministry of Dr. Allen Jones. After graduating from Temple Christian Academy in Lebanon, Ohio, he met and married his wife Jessie in 2006. They have two children, Greenlie and Leland. While attending Bible college at Andersonville Theological Seminary, he was called to preach and currently serves under Pastor William Burrows at Fellowship Baptist Church in Lebanon, Ohio, home of the Fellowship Tract League. The Lucas Watkins Family serves the Lord in teaching, preaching, and singing conservative God-honoring music for church, revival meetings, and special services.